Performance Improvement in Public Service Delivery

Performance Improvement in Public Service Delivery

A tool-kit for managers

Lynton Barker and Rom Rubycz

PITMAN PUBLISHING | Coopers &Lybrand

PITMAN PUBLISHING
128 Long Acre, London WC2E 9AN
Tel: +44 (0)71 447 2000
Fax: +44 (0)71 240 5771

A Division of Pearson Professional Limited

First published in Great Britain 1996

© Pearson Professional Limited 1996

The right of Lynton Barker and Rom Rubycz to be identified as Authors
of this Work has been asserted by them in accordance
with the Copyright, Designs and Patents Act 1988.

ISBN 0 273 61663 3

British Library Cataloguing in Publication Data
A CIP catalogue record for this book can be obtained from the British Library

10 9 8 7 6 5 4 3 2 1

Typeset by Phoenix Photosetting, Chatham, Kent
Printed and bound in Great Britain by
Biddles Ltd, Guildford and King's Lynn

The Publishers' policy is to use paper manufactured from sustainable forests.

Contents

Acknowledgements

This book is based on our practical experience of working with our clients and discussions with many of our colleagues at Coopers & Lybrand. We are grateful to them all for their thoughts and contributions.

Peter Williams, David Harper, Richard Clarke, Mark Hixon, Mike Gibson, Chris Sharp and Peninah Thomson made significant expert contribution to individual chapters. Thanks also to Barbara Shore for cartoons.

Foreword

Performance improvement is a common aim in both the public and private sectors: managers are always searching for ways to cut cost while increasing productivity and quality of service to customers. To support this, a number of management tools have been developed to assist managers to address specific performance issues.

Working closely with public sector managers, we have used a range of performance improvement techniques which have been tried and tested in the private sector. Drawing on private-sector experience can be beneficial but the public service manager needs to be discerning in choosing from the many options available.

To help simplify the choice and cut through the jargon, we have compiled an overview of the most useful of these techniques. These are explained in the following chapters and are intended as a menu for managers.

We hope you find the book informative and useful in deciding how to improve performance in public service delivery.

Lynton Barker and Rom Rubycz

Introduction

THE POSITION FACING PUBLIC SERVICE MANAGERS

Public service leaders throughout the world now expect public service managers to replicate the best concepts of continuous improvement, innovation and world class performance.

This book describes a range of performance improvement techniques used extensively in the private sector and which can help to improve performance in public sector service delivery. The book is designed to help you understand what lies behind the jargon that often clouds a set of simple but sensible ideas.

We have concentrated on those management tools which, in our experience, have proved most effective. The tool-kit covers:

- Business process re-engineering (BPR);
- Benchmarking;
- Activity based management (ABM);
- Priority based budgeting (PBB);
- Competition and partnerships;
- Change management processes.

Sometimes more drastic action is needed and simply addressing cost or service issues may not be enough. Instead the organisation may need to stand back and reassess its strategic direction, vision and position in its market or environment. In effect this often needs a form of 'Corporate Transformation' and we have set out in Chapter 9 our framework for such a transformation. If your organisation needs such a radical review or you are trying to create the environment for major change then you should read Chapter 9 before selecting any of the individual tools.

This book has evolved through developing and refining performance improvement methods with our colleagues and by working in partnership with our clients. Each chapter sets out one approach and is designed to stand alone as a brief introduction to each method. Enough information is provided in each case to offer an insight to the technique and will enable you to decide whether it will meet your particular needs.

CHAPTER 1

The performance improvement options

INTRODUCTION

There are a number of possible routes to improving an organisation's performance. These can be summarised as:

- **the 'external' route** – uses the stimulus of private sector involvement, whether through a market test, privatisation, or private/public sector partnerships.
- **the 'internal' route** – uses process improvement techniques such as BPR, ABM, benchmarking and so on.
- **a hybrid** – which combines the first two. For example, partnerships frequently act as a catalyst for internal performance improvements; or benchmarking can be used to determine whether a market test would be worthwhile.

The choice of route is complex and often confusing. The wrong choice can result in serious problems:

- failing to make the necessary changes;
- producing 'improvements' which the business does not really need, or producing them at unnecessary cost;
- damaging, rather than improving efficiency and customer service;
- losing control of the quality and timeliness of the output of key activities;
- undermining or even destroying existing improvement programmes;
- wasting staff time and damaging commitment and morale;
- wasting management time and damaging credibility.

This chapter and the next will enable you to understand the different options for performance improvement, and the implications of each. They will help you to match these with the requirements of your organisation and its current position, and so to tailor an approach which will meet your specific requirements.

EXTERNAL OR INTERNAL APPROACHES?

In the past, the level of competition and outsourcing has been driven by legislative and political requirements, rather than business needs; the agenda has been driven by more than just the requirement to improve performance. This situation may now be changing. For example, we know that in most economies government departments are asked to select whatever combination of internal and external measures best meets their requirements.

The external approach

As Table 1.1 shows, external approaches to performance improvement can have a number of advantages. They generally produce some form of cost or quality improvement, or both, and in the process of 'changing the rules' they often energise staff creativity with beneficial results.

However, the scope for the external approaches to improve performance is capped by what the private sector has to offer. The market for a service may not be well developed, or the in-house operation may already be efficient and effective. In such cases, the private sector may not be able to improve on the performance already available, or at least sufficiently to justify the costs of the exercise.

External approaches also risk a loss of control. Without adequate service specifications, one can lose control of the performance of key functions; and piecemeal outsourcing can fragment organisations making them difficult to manage coherently. External approaches can also lead to a net increase in bureaucracy, around the customer and supplier roles. Finally there is the increasing problem that in many areas of the public sector most of the 'obvious' areas for the external route have already been identified.

The internal approach

Turning to internal approaches, these can achieve the same performance improvements as the external approach (and often significantly better); and they are arguably more flexible in meeting the specific requirements of each organisation. They can be used to improve the performance of the whole organisation, and not just the parts market tested or outsourced. Finally, they do not run the same risks of loss of control that accompany external approaches.

The main disadvantage of the internal approach is that it frequently fails to deliver the intended results. This can happen because the wrong approach is chosen – the choices available are bewildering and are returned to in the next section. However, even with the right approach, it is easy to underestimate

Table 1.1 Market testing/outsourcing vs 'internal' approaches

	External route: market testing/outsourcing	'Internal' approaches
Advantages	• a known quantity • delivers cost and, potentially, service quality improvements • often frees staff creativity and energy in the course of the process • the result is final – there is no opting out • less need for continual management commitment • change management problems are reduced – there is no option but to change	• can achieve the same results as Route 1 or better • can transform the whole organisation, not just the parts market tested/outsourced • easier to tailor to the requirements of the organisation • no risk of loss of control through loss of ownership
Disadvantages	• beginning to run out of obvious areas – the remaining areas may be difficult to define or there may be no private sector alternatives • can lead to loss of control of key functions • can fragment organisations, so making co-ordination difficult • can increase contracting and customer/supplier bureaucracy	• the choice of internal techniques can be confusing as they overlap and duplicate each other – but they deliver very different results • frequently fail to deliver the required result, due to failure to change the culture • requires oversight and continuous senior management commitment, especially during implementation

the significant levels of management time and commitment required to make internal changes *happen*. With outsourcing, as stated, the process takes over and should deliver 'a result', come what may.

Criteria for choosing the external or internal approach

It should be apparent from Table 1.1 that neither internal nor external approaches are *necessarily* better. The route to performance improvement needs to be chosen according to the context and circumstances in each case. Table 1.2 identifies some of the criteria which need to be considered when making that choice. Table 1.2 identifies separately the external approaches of market testing, outright privatisation and partnerships, and internal approaches generally. (Different types of internal approach have not been identified separately at this stage: they are discussed in more detail in the next section.)

The list of criteria in Table 1.2 is not exhaustive, although it covers many of the situations typically encountered in the public sector. Table 1.2 shows that:

- external approaches tend to be best suited to non-core activities and services, where there is no risk from the loss of direct control and where the service provided tends to be easy to specify. They naturally assume that the private sector is capable of delivering the performance improvements required;
- they might also be used where the level of restructuring required exceeds internal skills and capacity, or is simply not worth the cost. In such cases, one might seek either to privatise the activity altogether or to import the necessary skills via a partnership with the private sector;
- internal approaches are more suitable for activities which are critical to business objectives, or where the organisation is significantly at risk if the activity fails: it is likely to be strongly preferable to retain internal control over these;
- internal approaches are also more suitable for activities which are difficult to specify, and where volumes and service requirements may be subject to change and hence unclear. In either case there may be difficulty in framing an operable contract;
- private/public sector partnerships can offer a 'half way house' where there are strong pressures to use the external route but where issues of risk and control remain. They can also be used as a means of importing private sector skills where these are required.

These criteria are only guidelines, and it is possible to point to examples which apparently contradict some of them. For example, many organisations in both the public and private sectors are outsourcing their IT activities

Table 1.2 Internal, external and partnership options

Criteria	External (market test)	External (privatise)	External (partnership)	Internal
The activity is core (strategically significant) to the achievement of business objectives				√
The activity is core, but requires investment which cannot be provided internally			√	
There is a high risk to the organisation if the activity fails			√	√
The activity is difficult to specify measurably				√
The activity is small, perhaps with a declining workload				√
Workloads are fluctuating and difficult to predict			√	√
The activity and/or its customers are undergoing rapid change – future service requirements are unclear			√	√
The activity is peripheral to the main mission – perhaps managed as a service or an overhead	√	√		
It is difficult to attract the required calibre of staff	√	√	√	
There is a need to mix private sector skills with those already in-house			√	
The activity requires significant restructuring, requiring disproportionate cost or effort		√	√	
Existing practices are entrenched and may not be easy to change	√	√		
Senior management attention and commitment may not be strong enough to drive through internal change	√	√		
External suppliers exist for the activity in question	√	√	√	
The activity is already competitive and would benefit from access to wider markets			√	
The performance level required is close to or exceeds that available from the private sector			√	√

despite the risk to their operations if the activity fails. In such higher risk cases, if the contracting organisation is wise there will be clear service level agreements and an evaluation of back-up capacity so that the likelihood of the *activity* actually failing completely is remote.

However, this is to touch upon a very big subject, and one that is outside the scope of this book. The focus here is on outsourcing as a performance improvement technique, and not on the mechanics of service specification or contracting. The next section therefore turns to selecting the appropriate, or internal, approach. Your outsourcing contractor is likely to be using the same approaches as those described in the next section to improve the performance of the functions he takes over!

Which internal approach?

There are many – too many – internal approaches to improving the performance of your organisation. Benchmarking apart, most of them have their own acronym – BPR, ABM, PBB, and so on – and most have at some point been hailed as the latest (or last) word in management thinking. The choice of approach is difficult and confusing, and matters are not helped by the consequences of getting the choice wrong.

Are you a cynic or a fashion follower?

Not surprisingly, managers seeking to improve the performance of their organisations tend to respond with one of two views:

- the 'cynical' view: the choice of approach doesn't matter since they are all basically the same thing (applied common sense), dressed up in different ways;
- the 'fashion follower's' view: a desire to try a technique because it is new and fashionable. At its worst, this view can become an uncritical acceptance of the latest management fad. At the time of writing the fashion is probably still for business process re-engineering (BPR), but with benchmarking coming up fast in the rear view mirror. In the recent past the fad was zero-based budgeting techniques such as priority based budgeting (PBB).

There is some justification for both views. The cynic would point out that the differences between the definitions of the various approaches available have always been exaggerated, partly by those selling them in order to differentiate themselves from the competition. Such valid distinctions as there are have become blurred through incorrect usage.

The fashion follower would respond that the different approaches have different objectives, and tend to achieve different results. There is again some

justification for this position. Paradoxically, in the light of the cynic's view above, BPR *is* different; it *is* more radical. Benchmarking *is* particularly relevant at present, in helping to address what for many managers is currently a real issue: whether to use the external approach to improve the performance of their organisations, or whether to seek the same improvements via in-house resources.

Internal approaches: separating the labels from the underlying reality

Despite the grains of truth in each of their viewpoints, both the cynic and the fashion follower are wrong, and their performance improvement initiatives would probably fail. The key to the argument is to differentiate between:

- the overall approaches;
- the tools and techniques which make them up.

As the cynic has realised, most internal approaches use (and have always used) a similar kit of tools and techniques. However, each approach *con-*

figures these tools and techniques differently, in order to meet very different objectives and deliver dramatically different results. Each will be appropriate at different times and in different circumstances.

It is therefore risky to opt for an approach in the belief that one is as good as another, or conversely because it is the latest management fad. To choose the relevant performance improvement approach, therefore, managers need to understand the precise requirements of their organisation. You will need to answer such questions as:

- Which performance improvements are required? How large are they?
- How much of the organisation is involved? When are the improvements required?
- How critical are the improvements? What level of risk needs to be incurred?
- What is the starting point – how good is current performance, what information is available, what other initiatives are going on?
- What might prevent improvements being achieved, and how can this be managed?

The next chapter identifies some thirty such questions whose answers could have a significant bearing on how performance improvements should be sought. Only when the answers to these are known and agreed should an approach be selected.

Selecting an approach – the options available

To make that selection, a clear understanding will also be required of what each approach seeks to achieve, and the circumstances in which it might be appropriate. The following approaches are discussed below:

- business process re-engineering (BPR);
- activity based management (ABM);
- priority based budgeting (PBB);
- benchmarking.

Business process re-engineering

BPR aims at *radical* improvements in cycle time, service levels and quality in *core business processes*. In improving these aspects, BPR frequently delivers major cost savings at the same time. 'Radical' changes in this context might include:

- elimination of entire processes;
- re-modelling of entire processes or businesses, typically to take advantage

of new business philosophies, to meet new perceptions of environmental threats and opportunities.

These changes are usually 'one-off', rather than continuous improvements; BPR is thus a review and re-design technique and not a technique for ongoing management.

A 'process' is a set of linked activities which provide an output. Processes probably flow across existing functional boundaries within the organisation, such as finance, registry, case management and so on. They will quite possibly flow between organisations as well. One complex example of this is the criminal justice system in the UK, where processes can flow between the Lord Chancellor's Department, the Home Office, different police forces, Crown and Magistrates courts, solicitors, barristers, DVLA, Social Services, Immigration, the Prisons department and others!

A 'core' process is one which directly addresses the needs of customers, or which is critical to the organisation's capability to deliver a service. Improvement in these would transform the service or value which the organisation delivers, and therefore has potentially a greater beneficial impact. For example, in a casework-based organisation, case determination and appeals might be core processes, as these have a direct impact upon the customer. Fact finding (even if it involves asking the customer questions), and overheads such as copying and reproduction (for example) would not; these are simply the price of being in the 'case work business' in the first place.

Typically a BPR exercise might consist of:

- mapping existing processes;
- collating views and observations on problems experienced;
- deliberately thinking as laterally as possible about how the process might be improved – whether it is needed at all, or whether its objectives can be met in completely different ways;
- designing new processes;
- developing the detailed procedures, job descriptions and so on required to make the process 'real';
- testing the processes, and if appropriate, new IT systems to support it;
- implementation.

Project management, internal communications and change management would need to be constant throughout. BPR exercises tend to take longer than would some of the other approaches if applied to the same area of the organisation, because the level of change which results tends to require more preparation for its implementation; however, the approach generally allows for 'quick wins' to be identified and thus some short-term benefits to be gained.

It is important in BPR to examine and re-engineer each process from end to end, taking in the chain of contributions to it (the value chain), and not be constrained to look within each organisational function involved. It is also important to deliberately think as laterally as possible when generating ideas for new processes, and not to be constrained by existing business methods and procedures, or existing IT systems. (Opportunities provided by IT developments can indeed be the catalyst for a BPR exercise.) By ignoring existing constraints in this way, BPR produces potentially the most radical changes of any performance improvement technique in Route 1 or Route 2.

Equally, however, the level of change which BPR engenders – it has been likened to re-designing an aeroplane in-flight – means that the risks associated with it can be considerable. It often entails:

- a significant re-definition of the organisation away from traditional functions to support the business processes which it defines;
- a complete re-casting of business methods, practices and relationships;
- a radical re-appraisal of existing IT systems to support the proposed process changes. (Many of the early proponents of BPR in the market place were IT vendors.)

Operational effectiveness can be damaged if these changes are inappropriate; and even if they are appropriate, they may be so radical and so wide-ranging that they cannot be implemented. At the very least there is likely to be a requirement for very significant management involvement and commitment if the changes are to be seen through.

To summarise, BPR is suitable where:

- there is a compelling need for major change – your organisation is on what is sometimes referred to as the 'burning platform'. This platform must justify the greater risk and dislocation;
- there is however time to develop, think through and prepare for radical change;
- there is a willingness to think laterally – to come up with entirely new ways of carrying out a process, or entirely new methods of organisation;
- there is strong, visible and continuous commitment from the top of your organisation downwards, until implementation is complete;
- there is scope to identify and make the changes required. For example, there is no point in doing BPR as one of a number of change initiatives in the same area; there must be complete access to the core processes; and there must be sufficient freedom of action delegated from any higher authority to make the radical changes required;

- the people in your organisation can be persuaded and motivated to make radical changes.

Activity based management

ABM provides a structured approach to assessing, targeting and managing the performance of organisations. It relates resources (costs) to products or services delivered to customers. In so doing it addresses both cost containment and service improvements, although arguably the former tends to receive the greater emphasis. Improvements which ABM typically (though not always) identifies might include:

- elimination of waste;
- streamlining workflows;
- reducing unused capacity;
- addressing the root causes of unnecessary costs.

It can be applied to the whole organisation, but it has been used particularly successfully in government to improve the quality and reduce costs of internal services (overheads). This contrasts with the focus on core processes which is the hallmark of BPR. The structured nature of the approach is often seen to strike the right note within public sector organisations, although the downside of this is that it can be quite labour intensive.

As its name implies, the primary focus of ABM is on individual activities, and the contribution which each makes to the final product. The core of its approach is the management accounting technique of activity analysis. This allows the identification of:

- **cost drivers** – the factors which require expenditure on the activity in question (for example, the cost drivers for an inspection activity might be the error rate and the number of inspectors);
- **value-adding** and **non-value-adding** activities, by reference to whether their elimination would materially reduce the performance, function, quality and value of the product or service, as perceived by the customer. ('Customer' in this context can be internal or external.)

ABM then supports the restructuring and focused management of those activities. It uses the information and quantification gained for planning and targeting performance, and thus for preventing performance variations from occurring. To this extent, ABM provides a management framework for continuous improvement, rather than a one-shot review of the kind that BPR offers. It tends, 'quick wins' apart, to allow the change programme to commence sooner than would BPR.

ABM is capable of taking an end-to-end view of business processes (individual activities are, after all, the building blocks of processes), and it is accordingly capable of identifying improvement opportunities both within and across business functions. However, it tends to remain within functional boundaries. It is also applied at a lower-level, more detailed and more quantitative analysis of the existing situation than would be expected of BPR. The latter tends to work at the level of end-to-end processes as they will become, with less analysis of the existing situation at the individual activity level.

ABM also tends to identify improvements within the framework of business processes which are already in operation. It is therefore less likely to produce radical suggestions for dispensing with the process altogether or transforming the entire approach to the work in question, in the way that, say, BPR might. Thus, it is less inherently risky than BPR; but equally it is more likely to produce incremental changes. Choosing between the two approaches demands a careful balance of the degree of risk and the type of change which the situation demands. BPR could incur higher risks than is necessary; ABM could fail to make changes of the magnitude required.

ABM is therefore most appropriate where:

- there is no need to run the risks of more radical changes;
- reduction and more effective management of costs, in particular overhead costs, can make a significant contribution to the business (albeit that service improvements may also be required);
- there is a requirement for a management framework within which to achieve continuous improvements;
- its relatively structured nature is perceived to be culturally and organisationally appropriate.

However, although ABM tends to produce less radical, more incremental changes, the requirement for management commitment to *implement* the changes identified is just as critical. A change may be 'incremental' from the perspective of the organisation, but revolutionary and threatening to the individual(s) affected. They will need to be led, communicated with, persuaded, trained, and reassured in ABM just as for BPR-generated changes. Indeed, there is an argument that BPR changes can be easier to make, because BPR tends to be used in situations where the organisation has little choice but to make changes.

Priority based budgeting

PBB traces its ancestry to the zero-based budgeting with which many organisations experimented in the sixties and seventies. It is a resource allocation technique which seeks to answer the question, 'how should my organisation best commit its resources to deliver its business objectives'. As such it seeks to address the shortcomings of traditional budgeting systems which merely reflect either organisational hierarchies, or worse, input line items (e.g. wages, vehicles, premises), and which prevent this question from even being approached.

Thus, PBB requires a thorough-going review of the budget 'base' – the proportion of committed expenditure which has built up year on year – in the light of the organisation's strategy and objectives. The budget is divided into 'subjects' or management units, which are required to demonstrate that their expenditure is required in order to deliver those objectives. Planning guidelines are established within which different service level options are generated by each subject, starting from a zero or near-zero base. Options are then prioritised to create an overall budget which conforms to the planning guidelines and which has in effect been tailored to the overall objectives. The budget is then free of the distortions and dead weight of expenditure which is committed 'because it has always been', having long outlived its original rationale.

In achieving this, PBB turns the budget into a key management tool. Service levels and costs developed as part of each option package can be used to establish performance indicators and targets to support performance monitoring during the year.

Although its particular focus on the resource allocation process is unique, PBB is closely related to ABM in that it can also make extensive use of activity analysis in order to determine the value added by each activity. It tends like ABM to focus on cost reductions. However, the review process which it embodies frequently identifies opportunities for service improvements within the reduced budget ceiling; and it can be used to ensure that growth in expenditure as well as reductions take place in line with organisational priorities.

The application of PBB tends to be synchronised with the organisation's annual budgetary cycle. It tends to be used as a 'one-shot' budgetary review: it would be unusual to carry out a PBB exercise every year. This is because, unless the organisation has experienced significant and unforeseen change within the year, there is little justification for repeating it at one year intervals. Relatively little, in budgetary terms, would have changed. However, it would be feasible and sensible to conduct a rolling review covering, say, 20 per cent of the budget each year and thus the whole organisation every five years.

PBB can be either functional or process-orientated, depending on how budget subjects are identified. However, as most organisations are managed functionally, PBB tends to follow suit. This in turn ensures that it is less radical than a deliberately cross-functional approach such as that provided by BPR; typically, cost savings of 5 to 20 per cent are identified, although as noted, it is frequently possible to *improve* service levels within the reduced figure. Like ABM, PBB has been used with particular effect to manage expenditure on non-core items and overheads.

The approach is highly structured, and very participative. Budget managers are required to analyse their activities, outputs and resources, to identify possible improvements in their working methods, and to agree with their (internal or external) customers the impact of different service levels. This makes it labour intensive, and relatively time consuming (another reason why it would not be repeated for the whole organisation every year). However, it also helps to maximise involvement and staff 'buy in', which is in turn critical to implementing the performance improvements identified. Significantly in the public sector, it seems to work very well in political environments, because there are 'slots' where politicians can readily be integrated into the process in order to decide spending priorities.

Benchmarking

Benchmarking – comparing business performance with 'best in class' organisations – is one of the most widely used techniques for improving performance. Strictly speaking benchmarking is not a complete *approach* to performance improvement in itself, because having identified a performance differential, one would then need to use some other techniques to identify and implement the changes required to address this. For this reason, benchmarking more usually forms part of the kit of tools techniques used by the wider approaches discussed above, such as BPR, ABM and PBB.

However, benchmarking is included here because it is currently the subject of much interest in the public sector, and because the label is frequently applied to the subsequent process improvements as well.

Benchmarking is in effect used to identify the scope and quantify the size of the performance improvement required to become the best in class, and then to measure whether it has been achieved. Repeated benchmark measures can then be used to stimulate continuous improvements.

The technique can be applied at two levels:

- comparing performance *metrics* – 'does my organisation undertake function x cheaper/faster/etc. than comparable organisations?'
- comparing the underlying processes, structures and technologies, in an effort to explain *why* the performance differential has arisen. In such cases, benchmarking can be a valuable tool for sharing experience and best practice between organisations.

In either case, there are also decisions to be taken about the type of comparator organisation to be used:

- **internal benchmarking** – comparisons between different operating units (for example different, but similar, regional offices) in the same organisation;

- **external (within class) benchmarking** – comparisons between different organisations of the same type, such as between different local authorities or health trusts;
- **external (out of class) benchmarking** – comparisons with completely different organisations. Here one is deliberately comparing 'apples with oranges' to see what the comparisons reveal. As an example, it might be instructive to benchmark a process which assesses entitlements and awards grants or benefits against an insurance or actuarial back office.

Benchmarking can be either process or functionally based, depending on inclination and the availability of comparators; and it can focus on either core or support processes. Similarly, it can be geared equally to cost or service level and quality comparisons. It may identify the scope for incremental or radical performance improvements, again depending on the comparators used. Clearly, for organisations which are already approaching the best in their class, it has limited potential, unless an external (out of class) benchmark identifies further opportunities.

Benchmarking has a number of potential pitfalls. Particularly where processes are being benchmarked it may be difficult to identify organisations which offer a meaningful comparison. As with any performance improvement approach or technique, it is possible to waste a good deal of effort measuring and improving the 'wrong' things; there needs to be a clear view of which performance improvements the organisation actually *needs*, based on well defined strategic goals and objectives.

A third pitfall is the tendency to identify benchmarks with an excessive level of detail. Particularly for cost comparisons, it is easy to forget that benchmarking is not an accounting exercise: robust measures do not necessarily require costs to be reconciled to the nearest penny.

To summarise, benchmarking is not a complete approach to performance improvement in itself; it needs to be used in conjunction with one of the other techniques above to specify and *deliver* the changes required. One would expect to use benchmarking where:

- there is a need to establish performance levels relative to competing or similar organisations, in order to gauge the extent of improvements required;
- there is a need to maintain a climate of continuous improvement once the main exercise has been completed.

'Mixing and matching' – understanding the basic ingredients

It should be clear from the preceding section that while the different performance improvement approaches on the market are based largely on the same set of core techniques, they are configured to deliver different products, and widely different levels and types of change. However, the approaches just discussed are in effect archetypes; there are infinite possible variations on the basic themes. This means that you do not have to fit your organisation's requirements into one of a limited number of 'pigeon holes'; it is possible to tailor a performance approach which meets your specific requirements.

One form of tailoring is simply to combine two or more of the broad approaches set out above. The possibilities include (but are not restricted to) the following:

- **any approach with benchmarking** – as noted, all of the broad approaches above could potentially employ benchmarking as a tool;
- **BPR and ABM** – it would be possible to undertake a radical re-design exercise with BPR and then use ABM techniques for defining and controlling the cost base thereafter, and also for maintaining the stimulus for continuous improvement;
- **ABM and PBB** – given that these two approaches are based on the core technique of activity analysis, it would be possible to derive the basic activity structure using ABM, and then derive service level options for budgetary purposes using PBB.

A second form of tailoring is to look at the level below the broad approaches, and bespoke your own performance improvement initiative from the portfolio of basic techniques which underpins all the approaches. Indeed, many managers unknowingly do this anyway. For example, it is common in the public sector and elsewhere to find process improvement initiatives which use the process mapping and ideas generation techniques from BPR but to achieve more incremental results.

Bespoking your own approach from the underlying tools and techniques offers the greatest flexibility and the closest fit with the specific requirements of the organisation. However it requires, if anything, even greater clarity about why the organisation needs to improve its performance and about the constraints upon it. In the next chapter we set out a series of diagnostic questions which managers need to ask themselves in order to be sure of choosing the right techniques, adapting them appropriately, and successfully implementing the improvements identified.

CHAPTER 2

Choosing the best option

INTRODUCTION

Chapter 1 discussed the different broad approaches available to managers seeking to improve the performance of their organisations. This chapter sets out a diagnostic assessment designed to help in the choice of broad approach or, if required, the bespoking of an approach to meet a specific set of requirements. The assessment is developed from one used by Coopers & Lybrand in our work across the breadth of the public sector.

PURPOSE OF THE DIAGNOSTIC ASSESSMENT

The diagnostic assessment will help you to identify and agree:

- what changes are required;
- how radical they need to be;
- where they need to fall;
- what might stop them from happening;
- what tools and techniques you should consider using.

It takes the form of a series of matrices, within which the organisation's position and requirements are plotted on some 30 scales. Typically, it would be completed by a group of senior managers, possibly with input from the staff likely to be involved; this would normally take between half and one day,[1] although some questions, for example those on competition, may require a separate exercise.

When using the diagnostic assessment with our clients we find that the record of the outcomes is often the least important aspect. Much more critical is the discussion between those to be involved in making the changes, leading to an *agreed* assessment of the current position and requirements for moving forward.

WHY DO WE NEED TO IMPROVE OUR PERFORMANCE?

Figure 2.1 explores the *reasons* for improving the performance of your organisation. The matrix is based on those we encounter most commonly in working with our public sector clients; it does not list all the possibilities. You will need a shared understanding of what you are responding *to*, before you can frame the response itself. Without this there is a risk in some cases of investing effort in the 'wrong' performance improvements.

Today, by far the most common reasons are cost constraints, and/or public requirements for improved service delivery – the two pressures which formed the background to this book. Reasons 3 and 4 on the list will concern managers whose businesses already compete with the private sector, or are about to be assessed against the private sector yardstick. You will need to be clear where and how the competition is likely to have an impact, and thus exactly which dimensions on which you need to improve. Do you face competition on cost or service levels, or some combination of both?

Reason 5 will apply where there is a need to ensure that funds which may be available to expand a service are applied as effectively as possible. Reason 6 is different from the others in that it comes from the attitudes and approach of the managers and staff, rather than from some external factor.

Reason 7 is the ideal case: a business which is seeking to improve its performance in line with clearly articulated strategic objectives. Such an organisation will know which types of performance improvement it needs to achieve, where in its operations, why, and what the consequences are of failure. It is likely also to have co-ordinated other performance improvement exercises into a single programme.

When completing the matrix, try to prioritise the different possibilities shown, so that you arrive at an agreed view of the main reasons for change, and the relationship and interactions between each. For example, meeting short-term cost pressures or a survival threat posed by a market test can cut across the delivery of strategic objectives on which the long-term future of the organisation rests. How can both views be accommodated? In such a situation, one would seek to construct a programme of short term, rapid improvements which both meet the immediate requirement and provide the basis for longer term improvements. There are other types of interaction which you may need to consider, for example:

- the impact of legislative demands or requirements for an improved service within a reducing budget – achieving growth and managed contraction simultaneously;
- the impact of professionalism on reducing the willingness of staff to accommodate a reduction in service standards.

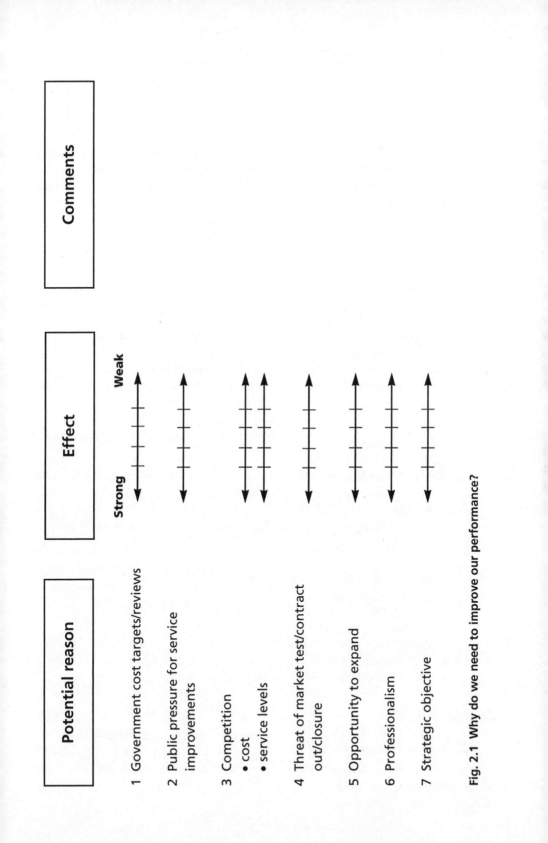

Potential reason

Effect

Comments

Strong   Weak

1 Government cost targets/reviews

2 Public pressure for service improvements

3 Competition
 • cost
 • service levels

4 Threat of market test/contract out/closure

5 Opportunity to expand

6 Professionalism

7 Strategic objective

Fig. 2.1 Why do we need to improve our performance?

WHAT IS THE NATURE OF THE IMPROVEMENT NEEDED?

Figure 2.2 seeks to establish the key parameters of the performance improvements required in your organisation, in terms of the type of change required, how critical it is, its urgency and so on. The different parameters addressed by the questions all interact, and do not necessarily point in the same direction. The resulting definition of the performance improvements required will therefore require a balance of the different factors involved.

What scale of cost reduction is required?
Where do we need to be?
What level of improvement is required?

These three questions refer to different aspects of the same overall issue, and are therefore discussed together.

It is critical to have some end-point, based on a clear business requirement, in mind when embarking on a performance improvement exercise. Perhaps surprisingly – the statement seems rather obvious – many organisations do not. They seek to improve performance by 'as much as they can', often with the tacit assumption that cost reduction or service improvement of any sort is 'a good thing' in itself. However, without an end-point to aim at they risk:

- investing time and effort, at high opportunity cost, in the 'wrong' improvements (for example reducing costs when quality improvements are the main imperative);
- possibly, incurring unnecessary risks through failing to make sufficiently radical improvements, or making changes which are more radical than may be required;
- not knowing when and whether they have succeeded (fear of being seen to fail may have been one reason for not identifying the end-point in the first place);
- having no way of prioritising different performance improvement activities which may be in progress;
- having no yardstick against which to balance the changes which may be proposed across the business as a whole;
- failing to make changes, through loss of momentum – without a clear target, with its own rationale, there may be no perceived reason to change, with the result that in most cases most people won't!

If your business has a clear strategy, then it should not be difficult to establish the type and level of improvements required, why, and also how long you have to achieve them. Equally, if you are responding to an external financial target the answers may also be clear! (However, the target itself is unlikely to help you when it comes to prioritising reductions in spending in line with business requirements.)

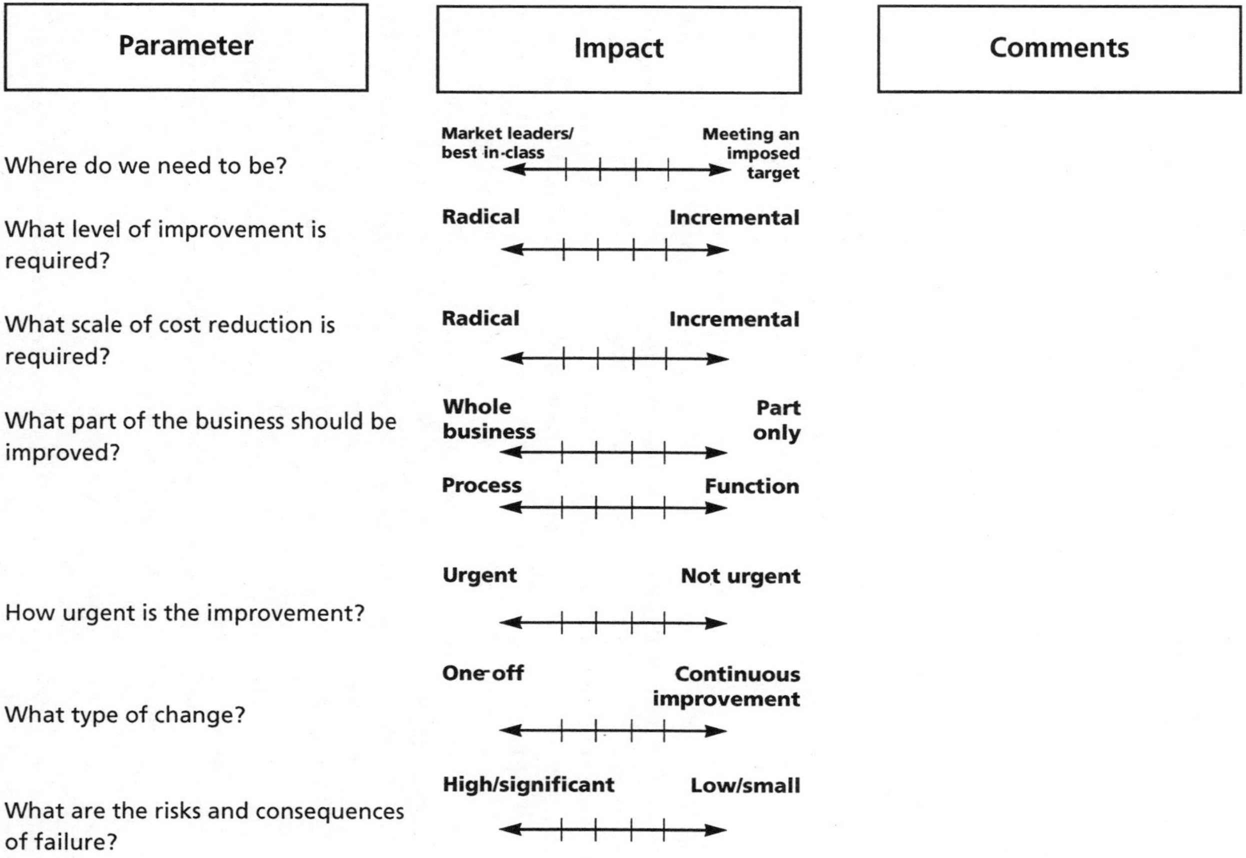

Parameter	Impact	Comments
Where do we need to be?	Market leaders/best in-class ←→ Meeting an imposed target	
What level of improvement is required?	Radical ←→ Incremental	
What scale of cost reduction is required?	Radical ←→ Incremental	
What part of the business should be improved?	Whole business ←→ Part only	
	Process ←→ Function	
How urgent is the improvement?	Urgent ←→ Not urgent	
What type of change?	One-off ←→ Continuous improvement	
What are the risks and consequences of failure?	High/significant ←→ Low/small	

Fig. 2.2 What is the nature of the improvement needed?

If you are seeking to ensure that you will survive a market test or remain competitive, or seeking to become the best in class, then you may need additional information about the yardsticks you will be assessing yourself against. One possibility might be some form of benchmarking exercise, if necessary through joining one of the many benchmarking consortia that exist, to obtain some quick comparative metrics.

Even if none of these situations apply, you will need some form of target based on a business requirement of what the organisation still does. You may therefore need to develop a set of service level and cost objectives based, say, on your customers' requirements, and then derive performance improvements from there.

What part of the business should be addressed?

Do you have a clear idea of which parts of the business should be improved, and equally, left alone? This may require some preliminary analysis of costs and quality achieved to identify the areas which are having the biggest impact on the operation as a whole. If there is time, a benchmarking exercise, perhaps focusing in the first instance just on metrics rather than analysis of the different processes involved (see Chapter 1) might be appropriate.

The issue of whether to focus on process or function will then depend on the scope of the improvements you are trying to make. If these relate to the cost or quality of the overall product of the organisation, then it is likely that a process view will be required. Concentrating on individual functions or departments would prevent the necessary end-to-end view linking all the factors affecting the cost and quality of the output. You would probably not identify opportunities to improve co-ordination and co-operation, and reduce duplication, between the departments.

The scope for the most radical improvements generally comes from taking a process view (it will be recalled from Chapter 1 that this is the rationale for BPR). However, you may wish to use process analysis techniques of the type employed by BPR, in order to obtain the clarity of view which BPR offers, but then to link these to a set of less radical ideas for changes to existing methods of doing business. This is in effect the approach being adopted by many public sector organisations today: whether or not they then *call* their approach BPR is irrelevant!

In general, only if the problems are clearly located in one part of the business would it make sense to take an organisationally based view. Even then, there will be a need to consider the interfaces between that part of the business and others which contribute to the same processes.

How urgent is the improvement?

There is a tendency to associate urgent improvements with more radical approaches such as BPR. In fact, unless they are simply imposed, radical changes will take more time, not less, as there is more preparation and change management groundwork required. If the situation really is urgent, common sense dictates that improvements should be targeted as specifically as possible: it is critical to form a rapid view of what does and, above all, does not need to be improved, and to concentrate your effort accordingly.

On the other hand, in the absence of an urgent external stimulus it can be difficult to generate the momentum required for sweeping improvements. If there is no 'burning platform', people may be disinclined to jump! In these circumstances, you may succeed in achieving more gentle, incremental improvements, but more radical changes will be rather harder; you would also need to consider the rationality of investing the greater time and effort, and incurring the greater risks that would be required, without due cause.

What type of change?

This question addresses the choice between a one-off set of changes and possibly restructuring, and a continuous improvement approach. (It is assumed that a single change which meets an objective is likely to be more radical than the incremental steps towards that objective achieved by continuous improvement.)

Answering the question requires you to balance a number of factors. First, what is the capability of your organisation to digest and act upon the results of a single, possibly more radical, set of changes? Second, and possibly conflicting with the first, there is the urgency issue discussed above – do you have *time* for a programme of continuous improvements? Will you get to where you need to be in time? Third, if you need to make radical improvements, will you sustain the momentum if these are programmed over an extended period, or should they be driven through as rapidly as possible?

The balance which needs to be struck will be unique to your organisation, and it is accordingly difficult to identify general points which can be made to help. However, some of the factors which need to be taken into account when considering the issue are set out in Figure 2.4 and discussed below. There is also the problem which many managers will face of not being able to draw conclusions until they know the *level* of change required – until they have identified in precise terms the problem(s) which need to be fixed and what this is likely to require. One way to address this is to tailor your approach to include an initial analysis of your environment (and the threats presented), current processes, current performance and relevant issues; then an overall approach can be selected depending on the level and extent of change found to be necessary. This initial review might or might not involve a brief benchmarking exercise.

What are the risks and consequences of failure?

What happens if you fail to make the performance improvements you need? How likely is this?

This issue needs to be approached on a number of levels. If there is an immediate threat to your business, say in the form of a market test, the presence of the 'burning platform' can be exploited to provide the *incentive* for staff to make the changes which will improve performance. The lack of a such a platform by definition implies that the immediate risk is lower, but as we noted earlier can reduce the scope for changing the way in which people actually behave, and thus the extent of the improvements which are possible.

Even if the incentive is present, however, one can still fail to make the right type and level of improvement. Strategies to manage high risk situations include:

- ensure that the lack of option but to change is widely and effectively communicated to staff within the organisation;
- endeavour to identify carefully the level of change required: you can neither afford too little or too much;
- more generally, attempt to match the level of improvement sought with the incentives for the organisation to change;
- identify as specifically as possible what might stop the required improvements being made (some possibilities are set out below), and invest effort in containing these risks.

WHAT SPECIFIC IMPROVEMENTS ARE REQUIRED?

This section of the diagnostic assessment explores the particular performance improvements which are required. Chapter 2 showed how the different broad approaches are configured to produce different products; your organisation may require some combination of the products shown (or others), in which case you will need to tailor your approach.

The list of possibilities shown in Figure 2.3 reflects our experience with our public sector clients; the list is not however exhaustive. The improvements most frequently sought are the first two (or in the case of an organisation which is already in a competitive market, the third). The remaining items are frequently sought in addition to one or both of the first two.

We regularly encounter organisations which embark on performance improvement exercises without being clear as to exactly what they want to achieve, and in particular the priorities they need to give the different possibilities. To which of the competing pressures on costs and service levels do you listen most attentively? Or again, suppose you are in competition with a private sector organisation: does your business actually *require* cost reductions, or should it seek to compete on quality? It is critical to be clear

Outputs	Priority	Comments/levels
	High priority · · · · · Low priority	
Reduced costs/improved efficiency	⟷	
Improved service levels/increased effectiveness	⟷	
Competitive advantage	⟷	
Improved budgetary process	⟷	
Prioritised services and reallocated resources	⟷	
Improved management information	⟷	
Comparative performance assessment (benchmarking)	⟷	
Skills/management development	⟷	

Fig. 2.3 What performance improvements are required?

about the *business need* for performance improvements, or you will invest effort in achieving the 'wrong' changes.

When identifying the results you want from your performance improvement initiative, you will therefore need to identify priorities, and also to balance these against factors already discussed, such as:

- the time you have available to make the changes;
- the willingness and ability of the organisation to assimilate the changes likely to be required;
- the level of risk incurred against the incentive to change.

The output you require from the performance improvement exercise will be critical when it comes to constructing your approach; the issue is returned to below.

WHAT IS YOUR STARTING POINT?

Figure 2.4 addresses the preparedness of your organisation for the changes which you may require of it.

What level of change has been/is already taking place?

This question is asked for two reasons. First, increasingly commonly in the public sector, the volume of change forced upon many organisations is almost overwhelming. Any further exercises involving major dislocation and changes in individuals' roles and behaviour may be more difficult to implement if those individuals are suffering from 'change fatigue'. Their ability to absorb and respond to the changes required is limited by their time, energy and commitment being pre-empted by other initiatives.

Second, and this is again common in the public sector, there may be so many piecemeal performance improvement initiatives that it is difficult to clarify the terms of reference of each. It becomes difficult to identify the impact which each is supposed to have, which takes priority and so on; the initiatives trip over each other. In one example of which we are aware, a central government department nearly market tested its invoice-paying function, thereby contractually setting its operation in stone, just as a BPR exercise and the application of electronic data interchange (EDI) would have rendered much of the function entirely unnecessary.

In both cases, the need is underlined for a clear direction for the organisation, and a clear set of priorities as to which improvements in performance are required, where, and why. It is then possible to construct a single, manageable programme of improvements – these may be using different approaches – which is at least co-ordinated and capable of avoiding duplication and/or internal conflicts.

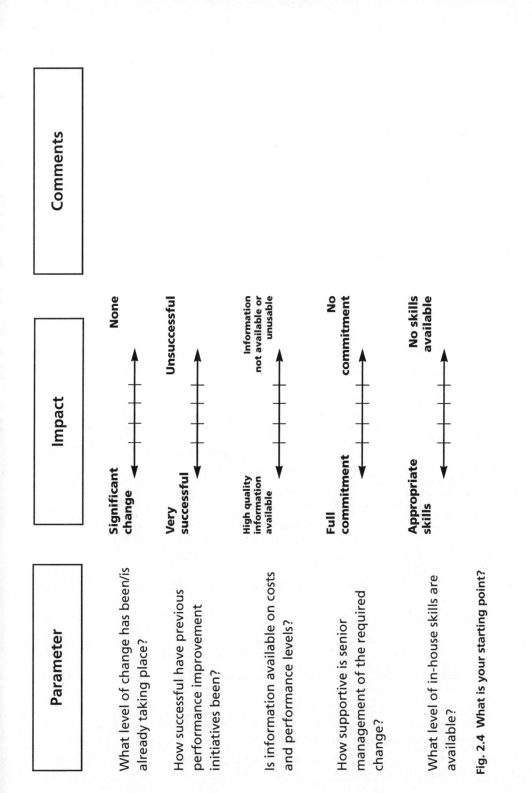

Parameter	Impact	Comments
What level of change has been/is already taking place?	Significant change ———— None	
How successful have previous performance improvement initiatives been?	Very successful ———— Unsuccessful	
Is information available on costs and performance levels?	High quality information available ———— Information not available or unusable	
How supportive is senior management of the required change?	Full commitment ———— No commitment	
What level of in-house skills are available?	Appropriate skills ———— No skills available	

Fig. 2.4 What is your starting point?

How successful have previous performance improvement initiatives been?

This question requires you to think about your experience of performance improvements to date. It also requires you to be honest, and so far as is possible, detached in analysing the reasons for past failures! If past attempts at change or performance improvement *have* failed, or only partially succeeded, it is self-evidently important to understand why, and how to avoid the problem recurring.

As a checklist to help your consideration of the issue, some possibilities are shown in Table 2.1.

Table 2.1 Checklist of possible reasons for failure of past performance improvement initiatives

	insufficient – or insufficiently demonstrated – and continuous management commitment:
	     lack of leadership and support for those making the changes
	     difficult decisions not made/path of least resistance taken

	insufficient communication throughout the analytic and implementation phases
	unclear terms of reference
	over-ambition – too wide a scope or too radical a change sought
	unclear priorities as to which performance improvements are required

	choice of the wrong approach:
	     the wrong techniques and tools
	     becoming bogged down in the detail

	insufficient planning for the implementation
	implementation took too long to demonstrate results

	insufficient attention to change management, and supporting staff as they make the change:
	     staff resistance
	     too many other changes simultaneously
	     insufficient incentive to change
	     too many 'stakeholders' – other parties with the ability to stop the required changes being made

	lack of experience and skills in the performance improvement techniques being used, and in implementation and change management
	made the wrong changes – e.g. service improvements which customers did not need, cost reductions which had unnecessarily adverse impacts on service levels
	poor targeting of benefits – lack of thought and clarity as to how the desired improvements should take effect
	conflict and overlap with other performance improvement and change initiatives

The opposite is also of course true. Where an initiative has succeeded, it is important to analyse what went well and why it succeeded, in order to try and learn from this. Be careful, though, that the previous exercise provides entirely relevant experience. Were all the external and internal circumstances the same as those you now face? If not, you may need to change your approach notwithstanding the success last time. Also, is the view that the exercise was an apparent success shared by all those who have been affected? If not, why not, and does it matter?

Having identified why a past initiative failed, ask yourself why this one should succeed. What will you do to address the reasons for the past failure? When answering, try to identify specific steps and avoid merely asserting the negative. For example, if management commitment was a problem last time, simply vowing to get more this time is unlikely to succeed. Why was it a problem? What specific actions will you take to ensure that it is not a problem this time?

Is information available on costs and performance levels?

All the performance improvement approaches discussed in this book will require some data on current costs and performance. This data is used to:

- identify the overall level of change required;
- identify 'hot spots' and target specific performance improvements;
- provide the baseline for establishing the extent of change actually achieved;
- in many cases, feed investment appraisals.

Cost and performance data is not always needed in great detail or within very narrow tolerances; indeed one of the biggest problems we encounter in working with public sector organisations is a tendency to seek too much detail and too high a burden of proof before making changes. However, seeking out or constructing cost and performance measures can be one of the most time-consuming and labour intensive aspects of any performance improvement initiative. Approaches such as ABM and PBB, which are based on activity based costing, and also benchmarking, will have the greatest overhead in this respect.

When planning you therefore need to be clear as to whether information is available on the right measures, to the right quality and at the right level of detail.

How supportive is senior management of the required change?

As has already been emphasised, strong, visible and continuous senior management commitment is the most critical success factor in any performance improvement initiative. It is not enough for the chief executive simply to issue a note at the start of the exercise and consider their involvement finished. Senior managers must:

- understand what is proposed;
- be seen continuously to be involved with the exercise;
- monitor progress and issues;
- be on hand to encourage and ensure that resistance is overcome;
- 'walk the talk' – if changes are required, they should be seen to make them first;
- communicate regularly their commitment to the initiative.

Even where there is no lack of willingness, the sheer amount of senior management time required is frequently underestimated. A recent study[2] into successes and failures in BPR concluded that the success of the exercise depends on executive level support and leadership. Do the senior managers in your organisation have the time to give the exercise the attention which is required? If not, the success of the exercise is very likely to depend on them re-arranging their commitments so that they do.

What level of in-house skills are available?

This question invites you to consider whether you have the skills required, in sufficient numbers and free of other commitments, to identify and implement the changes you require, in the time you have available. If you do not, you may need to recruit or second staff, or buy in the necessary skills. It *is* possible to learn as you proceed, but be certain that you can afford to fail first time around, as you may well do so!

USING THE DIAGNOSTIC ASSESSMENT

Having answered the questions in the matrices, you should have an agreed view of:

- why you are undertaking the performance improvement initiative;
- what specific improvements are required and where;
- how important and urgent they are;
- what might stop you making them;
- what other initiatives need to be co-ordinated to avoid conflicts and duplication;
- what has worked well and less well in the past, and the actions required to avoid past mistakes.

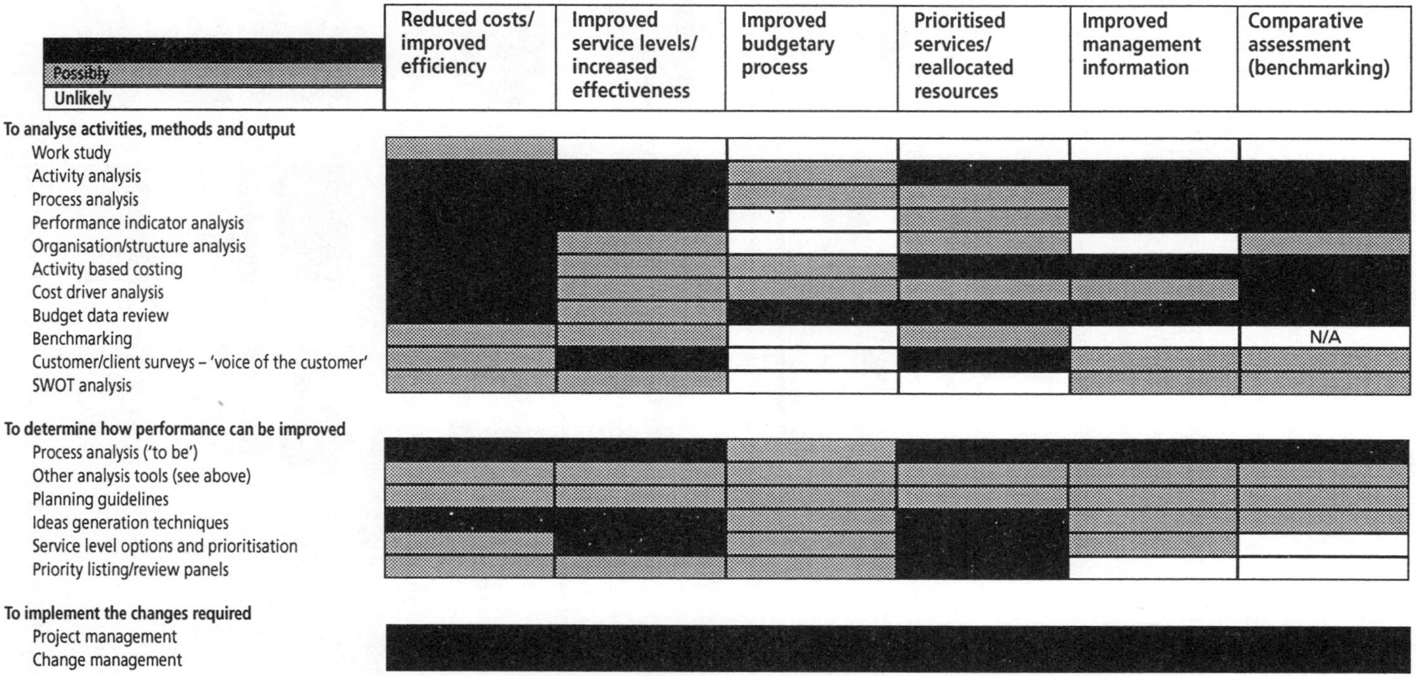

	Reduced costs/improved efficiency	Improved service levels/increased effectiveness	Improved budgetary process	Prioritised services/reallocated resources	Improved management information	Comparative assessment (benchmarking)

Legend: Possibly / Unlikely

To analyse activities, methods and output
Work study
Activity analysis
Process analysis
Performance indicator analysis
Organisation/structure analysis
Activity based costing
Cost driver analysis
Budget data review
Benchmarking (N/A)
Customer/client surveys – 'voice of the customer'
SWOT analysis

To determine how performance can be improved
Process analysis ('to be')
Other analysis tools (see above)
Planning guidelines
Ideas generation techniques
Service level options and prioritisation
Priority listing/review panels

To implement the changes required
Project management
Change management

Fig. 2.5 Use of techniques for performance improvement

Outputs and techniques required

The next step is to take the specific improvements required and from these, identify the particular techniques you might use. Figure 2.5 sets out the techniques which would *typically* be used to produce the deliverables specified in Figure 2.3.[3] The techniques in Figure 2.5 are described in more detail in Appendix A to this book.

Chapter 1 concluded by showing that the broad approaches it discussed could readily be combined into different configurations; it also noted that it was possible to bespoke an approach to meet the specific requirements of your organisation if none of the broad approaches suffice. By showing the

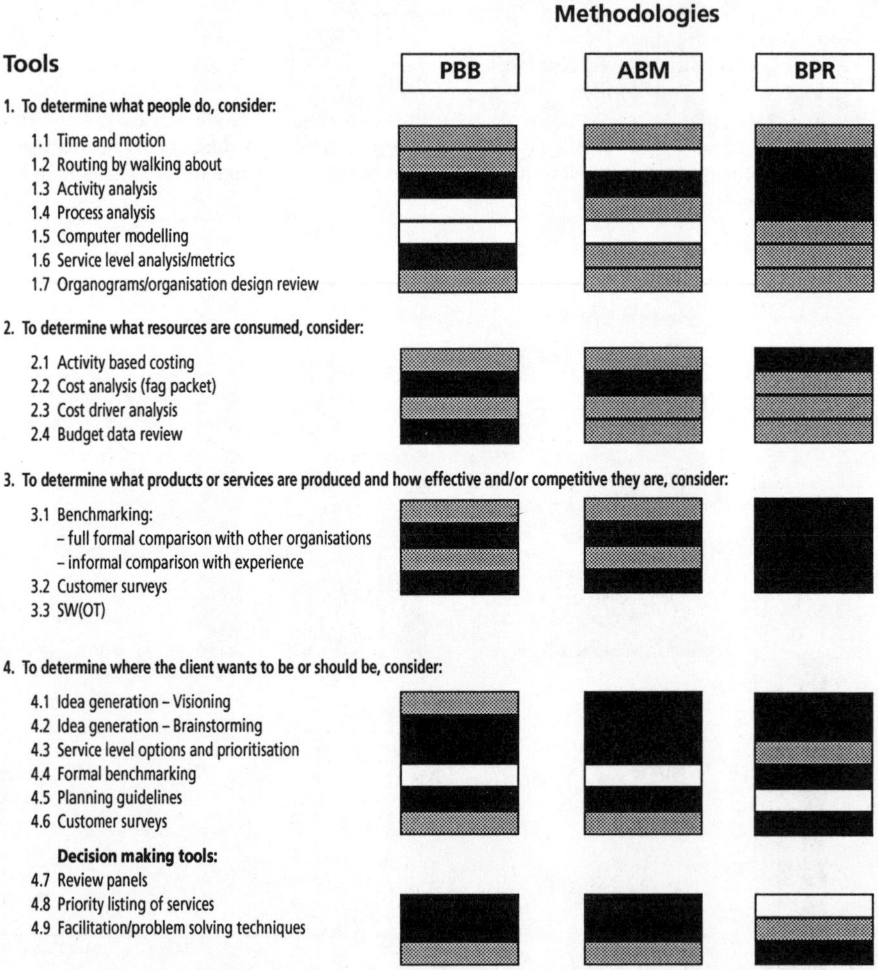

Methodologies

Tools

| | PBB | ABM | BPR |

1. To determine what people do, consider:

1.1 Time and motion
1.2 Routing by walking about
1.3 Activity analysis
1.4 Process analysis
1.5 Computer modelling
1.6 Service level analysis/metrics
1.7 Organograms/organisation design review

2. To determine what resources are consumed, consider:

2.1 Activity based costing
2.2 Cost analysis (fag packet)
2.3 Cost driver analysis
2.4 Budget data review

3. To determine what products or services are produced and how effective and/or competitive they are, consider:

3.1 Benchmarking:
 – full formal comparison with other organisations
 – informal comparison with experience
3.2 Customer surveys
3.3 SW(OT)

4. To determine where the client wants to be or should be, consider:

4.1 Idea generation – Visioning
4.2 Idea generation – Brainstorming
4.3 Service level options and prioritisation
4.4 Formal benchmarking
4.5 Planning guidelines
4.6 Customer surveys

 Decision making tools:
4.7 Review panels
4.8 Priority listing of services
4.9 Facilitation/problem solving techniques

Fig. 2.6 Performance improvement diagnostic matching tools to methodologies

specific techniques which one might use to deliver different types of performance improvement, Figure 2.5 supports this theme. It is intended to help you to begin to tailor your approach to performance improvement to your organisation's particular needs.

If the resulting approach is congruent with one of the broad approaches already discussed, well and good; if not, then it doesn't matter. However, for ease of reference, Figure 2.5 then relates these techniques to the broad approaches.

NOTES AND REFERENCES

1. Copies of the matrices used in the diagnostic assessment Figs. 2.1, 2.2, 2.3, 2.4 are available from Coopers & Lybrand.
2. For reference purposes see: *Best Practices in Reengineering,* Carr, D. K. and Johansson, H. J. McGraw-Hill Inc (1995).
3. Note that Figure 2.5 is *not* exclusive, and is intended to be indicative only; in practice the numbers of techniques available runs into the hundreds. No differentiation is offered between change management techniques, as they have the potential to apply equally to all required outputs.

CHAPTER 3

Implementing change

INTRODUCTION

This chapter explains why structural and procedural adjustments to organisations will not of themselves help managers in implementing the type of changes outlined in this book. It suggests three key issues that must be addressed by managers if they are to be successful in implementing the changes implicit in any environment, and introduces an organisational model that helps to diagnose the change management issue to be addressed. Finally, it examines the life cycle stages of the management of change, and the vital role of sponsorship in that process.

PREPARING TO MANAGE PUBLIC SECTOR CHANGE – THREE FUNDAMENTAL ISSUES

For senior managers, preparing to manage and implement change means doing three things:

1 deciding whether or not you believe that it is possible to manage change. If having considered this question you decide that there are actions that can be taken in managing change, then;
2 recognising that in British managerial culture (public or private sector) it is more usual to focus upon changes to structure and management process or procedure than upon changes in staff attitudes or organisational behaviour; and
3 accepting that because of this pattern, our skills as senior managers in addressing issues that relate to behavioural change are less honed and our experience less substantial.

A clear understanding of, first, one's own mind-set in relation to the possibility of managing change, therefore, is essential; and an appreciation of the fact that we are not necessarily playing to our strengths in seeking to manage behavioural as opposed to procedural change. Regardless of whether or not we are playing to our managerial strengths however, the magnitude of the changes facing the public sector means that the task of implementing them **must** be addressed and that all the components of the organisation – organisational culture, climate, and human behaviour as well as structure, processes and systems – will require attention if the change is to be systemic and not superficial.

WHY CHANGE PROJECTS FAIL

Reports and surveys published in 1993 and 1994 agree on the fact that very few major change projects (less than 20 per cent) deliver their promised benefits. The **symptoms of failure** are apparent: unclear goals, failure to communicate, lack of commitment, underestimated (and unaddressed) resistance to change, confused responsibilities, unforeseen difficulties, failure to monitor progress and to take appropriate corrective action.

The underlying and persistent **cause of failure** in change projects however rests with ourselves. We human beings are the most control oriented beings on this planet; we will vigorously defend the status quo in the face of significant and imposed change (even beneficial change) for fear that our own control, however tenuous, over the current situation might be lost. We are part of the problem: we must therefore form part of the solution. Implementing the changes taking place in the public sector needs, critically, to address not only the structural and procedural aspects but also the human aspects of change.

AN ORGANISATIONAL MODEL THAT BUILDS UNDERSTANDING OF CHANGE DYNAMICS AND AN ACCURATE DIAGNOSIS OF THE ISSUES TO BE ADDRESSED

Very often, change projects fail because they have been designed to address the presenting rather than the actual issue. The project ends up putting plasters on spots rather than curing the illness. Developing clear answers to the following questions is a crucial stage in establishing an agreed change vision:

- **what needs to change** to accomplish our mission?
- **in which ways** will we need to change the way we work?
- **who will** need to change, and in what way?
- **what else** in the organisation will need to be different, and in what way?

Figure 3.1 shows an organisational model (the Burke–Litwin model) we use to help leaders of organisations arrive at clear answers to these questions. The model is based upon general systems theory. The 'external environment' box represents the input and the 'individual and organisational performance' box represents the output; feedback loops go in both directions. The remaining boxes of the model represent the throughput aspect of general

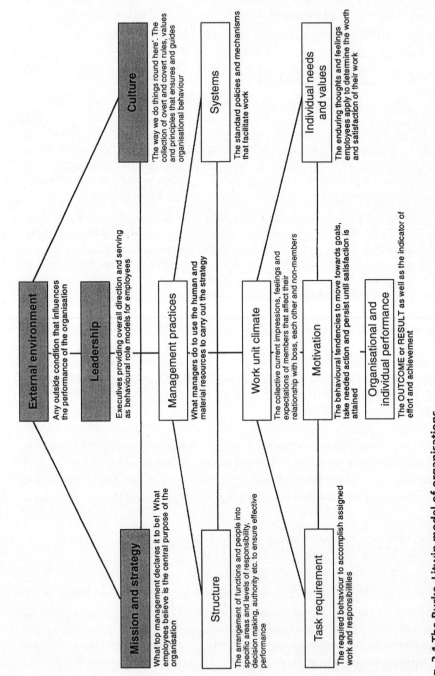

Fig. 3.1 The Burke–Litwin model of organisations

Source: Drawn from the work of W. Warner Burke and G. Litwin. *Journal of Management* (1992)

systems theory. The model is helpful in starting to think about the management of organisational change because:

- it shows how the various components of an organisation (any organisation) fit together;
- it makes clear that because of the linkages between the various components, change in one area will eventually have an impact upon performance, or practice, in other areas (the open-systems principle);
- it recognises the importance of the 'unseens' in organisations (culture; individual needs and values; motivation) by acknowledging them in the organisational hierarchy alongside the more commonly recognised components (for example structure; management practices; task requirement etc.);
- it is a causal model: for example, although culture and systems affect one another, culture has a stronger influence upon systems than vice versa;
- it differentiates between those components that are transformational (the hatched boxes – external environment, leadership, mission, and strategy and culture) and the remainder, which are transactional.

This last point merits interpretation. 'Transformational' refers to those areas in which alteration is likely to be caused by interaction with environmental forces (both inside and outside the organisation), and therefore requires people to have new behaviour patterns. In other words, transformational change requires a paradigm shift. The 'transactional' variables (those in boxes that are not hatched) are so called because an alteration associated with them takes place primarily through a relatively short-term reciprocity – an exchange – among people and groups within the organisation.

Using the Burke–Litwin model helps in diagnosing **what** an organisation needs to change; **how** it needs to change and **who** within it needs to change. It also defines the key levers that any organisation has available to work on in relation to making those changes happen. What using the model will not do however is tell you what to do to make change happen.

LIFE CYCLE STAGES OF THE MANAGEMENT OF CHANGE

As with any other process, a change management project goes through life cycle stages. These stages are never strictly sequential. New levels of data and awareness are progressively added and it is often necessary, for example, to revisit the goals of the change in the light of experience during implementation.

Working with senior managers on a change project (of whatever size) typically involves four stages:

- **assess** – defining the purpose and nature of change;
- **plan** – establishing an integrated behavioural and technical plan for change;
- **implement** – working through the process and the plan; building understanding and commitment to change and establishing new ways of working;
- **renew** – reviewing the entire process; adjusting in the light of performance; assessing achievement and learning.

In addition to the life cycle stages, there are three basic components, or 'change modules' that in our experience need to be included if a change implementation project is to be successful. Omitting any one of these will usually lead to failure of the project. They are:

- **change vision** – an analytical framework to assess what needs to change and why, and to establish a vision for change;
- **behavioural change** – a comprehensive set of diagnostics and methods for assessing behavioural risk factors and planning change processes to overcome them;
- **programme management** – tried and tested project management techniques and disciplines.

Figure 3.2 shows the life cycle stages and the change modules integrated in a Management of Change framework – *Taking Charge of Change* which brings together the best available diagnostic and planning tools and techniques to provide a powerful support to organisations managing the process and the content (of whichever type, technological, organisational, structural) of change.

Working on the three change modules, through the life cycle stages of the change project, provides managers with the **discipline** and the **comfort** needed for success: discipline, because observing the components of a clear framework ensures that no one component is inadvertently left out; comfort, because using a clear framework of proven efficacy provides a sense of security in what can often feel like uncharted waters.

FINALLY . . . SPONSORSHIP

The successful implementation of change cannot take place without an effective, committed sponsor.

The sponsor has to:

- have a position of status and authority;
- be personally committed to implementing change;
- demonstrate visible and sustained commitment;

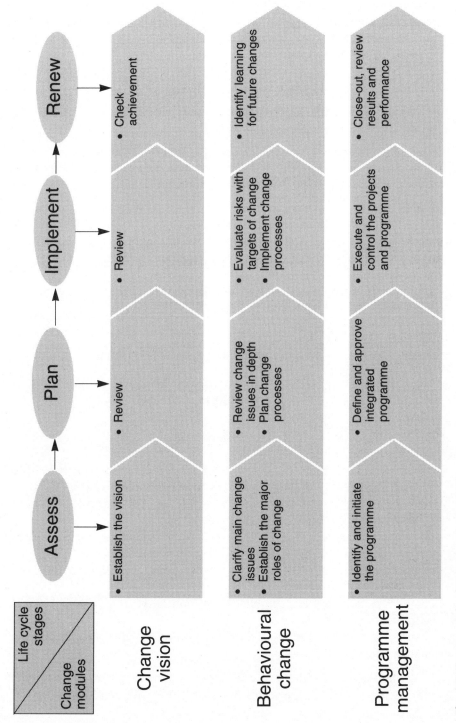

Fig. 3.2 Framework of Management of Change

- understand the dynamics of the change process;
- be able to interpret the pressures for change, the changes that are needed and the process that will be used to achieve them; be able to articulate them to his or her people;
- embody, in personal behaviours as well as in words, the changes he or she intends to implement in the organisation: 'walk the talk'.

With all the procedural components in place, a change project can still fail. Without successful sponsorship it **will** fail.

> a new idea either finds a champion or dies . . . no ordinary involvement with a new idea provides the energy required to cope with the indifference and resistance that major change provokes . . . Champions of new inventions display persistence and courage of heroic quality.

Edward Schon

What are the key actions that a committed sponsor should take to ensure that his or her change programme has the optimum chance of success?

- before introducing a major change, clarify the nature and scope of the project and the level of commitment required for its success;
- ensure that a tailored communication plan is developed for each key constituency affected by the change;
- ensure that an analysis is conducted of the organisation's capacity to assimilate the particular change;
- commit the appropriate amount of logistical, economic and political resources to the change to demonstrate the level of organisational commitment;
- devise a structured procedure to design the architecture necessary for successful implementation;
- ensure that all key individuals have been properly trained in order to fulfil their respective roles during the execution of the implementation plan;
- evaluate the nature and level of resistance or support to expect from individuals or groups that are the targets of change;
- assess the nature and level of stress that will be generated for those who are the targets of change when that change is introduced;
- assess the degree of resistance or support to expect from the culture of the organisation;
- ensure that progress and problems are monitored, and periodic formal reports are submitted;
- ensure that a final report is submitted regarding the ultimate status of the change effort.

Perhaps the most important thing to remember, for senior managers in the public or private sector preparing to embark upon the implementation of change, is that they are preparing to engage in a significant alteration to the dynamics of the organisation. In the final analysis this cannot be measured; nor can the course of it be accurately predicted. Implementing change requires skills different from those traditionally called upon by the management process; and a different approach. With the right skills, an appropriate approach, an empathy for the organisation and a degree of personal humility it is possible to undertake the implementation of change.

CHAPTER 4

Business process re-engineering

INTRODUCTION

Business process re-engineering (BPR) is undeniably trendy. It has probably attracted more attention as a tool for performance improvement than many of the other approaches discussed in this book and is currently one of the most talked about themes of modern management.

BPR is frequently portrayed as a means to achieve 'radical' change through a wide-ranging appraisal of business fundamentals. Not surprisingly, therefore, BPR's reputation has spread rapidly beyond the technique's roots in manufacturing and commerce.

Many public sector organisations have started to look at BPR to decide whether it has anything to offer in the performance improvement arena. The pressures on the public sector to improve performance stemming from:

- increasing expectations from the public of the services they receive;
- the opportunities provided by technology;
- the limited funds available

have already been discussed earlier in this book. BPR is a particularly relevant tool for delivering improvements led by these drivers. This is because BPR offers step change improvement – whether that be in cost or the quality of services provided.

ORIGINS OF BPR

Business process re-engineering has been defined as:

> The fundamental rethinking and radical re-design of business processes to achieve dramatic improvements in critical contemporary measures of performance, such as costs, quality service and speed.
>
> Hammer and Champy

Although the definition emphasises the radical nature of change that BPR strives to achieve, the approach itself has emerged from a range of approaches dating back as far as the 1960s.

The focus has moved from methods and procedures through systems to re-engineering as shown below.

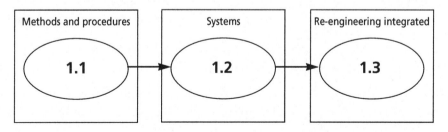

The re-engineering view is often perceived to be radical in its implementation for two main reasons:

- it focuses on processes which cut across existing functional boundaries;
- successful implementation depends on individuals within the organisation actually changing – their jobs, behaviours and attitudes.

There is also a perception that the private sector are more radical than the public sector. We examine these two perceptions below.

RADICAL CHANGE?

The public sector is no stranger to radical change. Policy changes at the centre of government affect radically the services to millions of people. The Inland Revenue are currently changing the tax assessment process – moving to self assessment. This will affect millions of taxpayers as well as impacting on the existing systems. Moreover, the poll tax could possibly be the largest failed attempt to re-engineer a process this decade (local tax collection is the process). So what can the public sector learn from BPR. The answer probably lies in the rigorousness of the approach, the checkpoints on the way that allow managers to identify and avoid potential failure and the containment of change to avoid risking the core purpose of the organisation.

The growth of the approach has led to the labelling of nearly all change as 're-engineering'. This has contributed to misunderstanding and confusion and has undoubtedly diverted organisations away from achieving the change they need.

For the purposes of this chapter a BPR project is characterised by being:

- holistic:
  - spanning the whole organisation, its people, functions and core purpose for existing;
- focused on core process:
  - concentrating on processes which deliver external customer needs;
- inclusive of a step change in perceived customer value:
  - whether the customer is a member of the public, a minister or another government department;
- explicit in the management of change:
  - without which BPR projects will fail.

This does not mean that readers should now stop if their project does not meet the above criteria. The remainder of this chapter outlines the essential principles of process re-engineering and suggests a series of 'golden rules' for success. So this is applicable to anyone involved with:

- process improvement;
- systems implementation involving process change and of course the BPR purists!

THE KEYS TO SUCCESS

Unfortunately, re-engineering an organisation is easier said than done. Success is not guaranteed. As with any other approach to business improvement, responding to the surrounding hype with a scatter of ill thought through initiatives can at best only achieve modest levels of success – if any at all. At worst, failure, disruption, expense and an erosion of faith in management will result.

The spur to persevere and get it right comes from re-engineering's rich rewards. In the private sector those companies that get it right really do benefit – lead time reductions of up to 90 per cent, 100 per cent improvements in customer service, and 50 per cent improvement in productivity have all been achieved. In the public sector major change implemented smoothly would be a feather in many caps.

So what does it take to join these organisations? Two overriding factors stand out. Firstly, by focusing on just a few key aspects in a business re-engineering programme, it is possible to reduce significantly the risk of failure. Identifying how many elements of an organisation can be tackled – and which precise ones, and in which order – is an aspect of re-engineering which is critical to success.

Secondly, it is vital for organisations to focus on re-engineering processes – because it is processes, rather than functional departments, which actually deliver benefits to the customer. Processes are rarely confined to a single functional department – so looking only at the operation of an aspect of a process within a department or function immediately loses sight of the greater whole. Sub-optimisation and duplication, result. That is why the term given to the approach is 'business process re-engineering'.

CAPTURING THE VOICE OF THE CUSTOMER

Almost by definition a business process re-engineering programme will claim a massive amount of effort. All too often, though, this resource commitment ends up being internally focused. There are many processes within an organisation, and a large proportion have no impact outside the organisation itself – financial management, recruitment, maintenance, property management, and so on. Clearly, re-designing any of these is likely to lead to reductions in non-valued-added activity and wasted effort, leading to consequent improvements in productivity and cost reductions. So much is obvious.

But the real prize is attained when businesses focus their efforts on those few core business processes which are most valued by its external customers. The fact that a business's recruitment processes are inefficient may not unduly worry most customers; but in contrast, inefficient processing of a benefits claim, or errors in the preparation of a new policy/legislation have serious implications to public sector management and politicians. By reappraising the ways in which these core processes are carried out, a business can dramatically change its capabilities – ideally, creating a shift in the value for money at which these processes deliver.

So when work starts on business process re-engineering programmes, this work should begin in the external environment, concentrating on those core business processes. It is essential to ensure that the voice of the customer is genuinely heard. Different situations require different techniques: one-to-one meetings, focus groups, surveys and structured workshops – all of these have their place. The purpose is the same – to understand, for both existing and potential customers, their expectations, their underlying needs, and which criteria most influence their perceptions of success.

This then leads to a set of re-engineering priorities being drawn up. More importantly, though, it can lead to the identification of potential step changes in performance – those transformations in customer-perceived performance that are so marked as to produce a significant and sustained increase in the organisation's performance. For example, an Executive Agency achieved a 50 per cent reduction in cost by repositioning the management of its records database under a single supplier who became totally responsible for development and maintenance. In the private sector a carpet fibre manufacturer achieved its step change by linking production with the retailer and the carpet mill so tightly that they were virtually one entity. Lead times, which were previously as much as nine weeks, were at a stroke reduced to one week.

WHAT ARE PROCESSES?

Any sequence of activities that takes place in order to get work done is a process. Processes range, in order of complexity, from something simple like writing a cheque, to functional, like maintaining an organisation's financial records, to cross-functional, like drawing up an organisation's financial plan.

A process may be . . .

Simple
    Taking a photograph
    Buying a radio
    Balancing your cheque book

Complex
    Developing film
    Buying a new radar system
    Balancing the budget

Every process receives inputs – that is, material from another source, such as invoices that have to be paid. Information is generally included with this material, such as an authorisation to pay an invoice. Once someone has received that information, a process transformation (which in this case includes all the steps involved in writing a cheque) can occur. That transformation, in turn, produces a product or service – the process's output.

Contrast this with a functional view of the organisation, which sees it in terms of its constituent parts, each of which carries out a specific task or range of tasks. It is rather like a production line. Raw material (people, requests, completed paperwork etc.) enters the organisation and passes through a sequence of discrete departments until the desired result is achieved.

The production line analogy is apt. Production lines and the functional focus share a common root in the principle of division of labour. Both are based on the belief that, by fragmenting work into numerous discrete elements, each can be carried out more effectively. As a result the task as a whole will be carried out more effectively.

Sadly this may not always be the case. When a single task is fragmented into several sub-tasks, or when the work of an organisation is spread among the number of departments, several things can happen:

- managers and staff lose sight of the overall purpose of the organisation and concentrate solely on their particular area of expertise or function. Nobody sees the 'whole picture' or is necessarily aware of how well the completed product or service meets the customer's needs;
- the entire operation proceeds at the speed of its slowest component. Delays at one machine in the production line, or hold-ups, in one department of the office, delay the whole organisation;
- communication channels need to be established to convey information, instructions or part-completed works between the various sections of the organisations. As a result there is scope for messages to become garbled or work to get lost as it moves around;
- buffer stocks of work build up at the interfaces between different parts of the organisation. In-trays (for paper) and waiting rooms (for people) are all too often the public sector's equivalent of the machinist's stock of 'work in progress'. Delays and errors inevitably arise as a result;
- staff loyalties can become distorted. People may come to care so much about their department and how well it is performing that they fail to notice broader organisational problems; or blame them on other departments. Feuding between functional departments is all too common; and often all too obvious when it impacts on customers.

The process view of an organisation looks first at what the organisation as a whole seeks to do for its customers. In doing so it ignores internal divisions and seeks instead to align the organisation's structure and ways of working with the needs of the people whom it serves.

SELECTING THE RIGHT PROCESS FOR RE-ENGINEERING

In many instances the right processes will select themselves as a result of listening to the customers. However it is useful to use the following generic core processes as a guide to their selection. These are:

- create a new policy or service;
- fulfil a customer need or request;
- win business (where executive agencies or Non-Departmental Public Bodies (NDPBs) have this as part of their mission).

Most organisations have a handful of core business processes. There are rarely more than 10. It can, however, be all too easy to allow the list to grow by including processes which the organisation itself believes to be core but which customers neither recognise nor value. In any case the re-engineering project is unlikely to succeed if more than a handful of processes are taken for re-engineering. On average the majority of projects take two or three processes forward for re-engineering.

There are many techniques which organisations can use to assist in the identification of its core business processes. These include:

- customer surveys;
- interviews with senior management;
- internal brainstorming;
- joint staff/customer workshops.

It is essential to ensure that all possible customers are covered, and that internal views are subjected to rigorous appraisal.

Identifying the core business processes is not always easy. It is important to understand clearly the core processes, however, since they will be at the heart of the subsequent re-engineering effort.

In addition, because the core process is at a high level and will contain many lower-level processes it is important to clarify carefully the input and output of the core process. A simple way to help with this definition is to return to the external customer and ensure that they are at each end of the core process. The table below provides some examples of the types of core processes which can be found within public sector organisations.

Core process	External customer	Inputs	Outputs
Managing a departmental budget	HM Treasury, PAC, NAO	Requirement to manage funds	Satisfied customer at HM Treasury, PAC, NAO
Hospital surgery service	Patient	Patient with a problem	Patient recovered

RUNNING AN ORGANISATION ON PROCESS LINES

It can be helpful to describe core processes in dynamic terms by reference to their inputs (the 'raw material' on which they work) and their outputs (the finished 'product' which they produce and which meets a customer's need).

A 'claims payment' process might take, as its input, a completed claim form. Following a series of evaluations, assessments, references to other databases etc., a decision is made on any payment due. The output of the 'claim payment' process is a transfer of money to the customer.

This simple example highlights some important features of a core business process:

- it may encompass several different functional departments (the front desk or post-room where claims are received, the records department where details of previous claims are held, the department responsible for assessing claims, the finance department which authorises payment and the cashier who issues cash);
- the output is of greater value to the customer than the input (clearly a cash payment is of greater value than a completed claim form, and even a decision to withhold payment provides 'value' in terms of clarifying the customer's entitlement);
- the process description is meaningful when viewed from outside the organisation ('claims payment' describes why the customer is in contact with the organisation whereas 'claims processing' and 'assessment' are unlikely to be cited as reasons);
- the process may extend beyond the existing boundaries of the organisation (e.g. the actual payment of cash may be carried out by a separate agency but is still, from the customer's perspective, part of a single process).

Note also that the names of functional departments are very rarely process descriptions:

- 'stores' is not a process, it is a department which carries out some tasks in a process called 'making goods available';
- 'radiology' is not a process, it is part of a 'diagnosis of disease' process;
- 'records' is not a process, it is a functional department which holds and supplies information to help front-line staff meet clients' needs;
- 'finance' is not a process, it too is a support function of little or no interest to customers.

Once the organisation's core business processes have been identified it can be helpful to consider:

- which functional departments are involved in carrying out each process;
- who, if anyone, 'owns' the process and is responsible for its overall effectiveness (in a typical functionally orientated organisation process ownership is unlikely to be recognisable);
- how can the performance of the process be measured (in terms of cost, quality, and productivity)?

A clear understanding of core business processes will help to ensure success in the next key stage of the BPR project when re-engineering to improve performance takes place.

In its purest form process view assigns responsibility for meeting a customer's needs in full to a single individual (or small group of individuals) within the organisation. Thus, instead of passing from department to department to obtain the service he/she requires, the customer of a process-orientated organisation can receive that service in its entirety by interacting with just one person or team. Similarly, in the case of paperwork, all decisions regarding an application, a request for information, payment, etc. are made by a single individual or work group.

Successful operation along process lines is not easy. It requires staff to have the skills and knowledge to deal with a much wider (and typically less predictable) range of tasks. In some cases it may also necessitate the establishment of multi-disciplinary teams whose members can work together in a flexible and responsive manner to meet customers' needs. Slavish adherence to procedural rules and strict demarcation of responsibilities along 'professional' or other lines is not feasible in a process-orientated organisation.

Clearly, it is not always possible or desirable to move to a wholly process-orientated approach to work in all areas of public service. Some tasks require specialist knowledge or access to sophisticated technical equipment which, by its very nature, cannot be operated by 'front-line', customer-facing staff. Individual's careers still depend on improving functional skills and the improvement of these skills needs a focus. In such cases, a degree of division of labour will inevitably persist, with certain key tasks continuing to be assigned to specialist departments. Nevertheless, a process approach can lower the barriers to accessing such specialist services or resources, often by assigning a member of staff to act as the customer's representative or advocate in doing so.

A practical example of where reorganisation has taken place to align with a process-orientated approach is the identification of a 'named nurse' in some NHS hospitals who is responsible for delivering (or co-ordinating) all aspects of an inpatient's care during their stay.

The named nurse will almost certainly act as a liaison point for doctors, paramedical staff and others whose skills are needed to provide the treatment required. In both cases, however, the customer's main point of contact throughout his/her interaction with the organisation is a single individual. He or she is not passed 'from pillar to post' with a risk of delay or loss of case notes.

PROCESS MODELLING

Once the core processes have been identified there is frequently a need to describe the processes. This description is required often for a number of purposes:

- to communicate to staff who work on the processes to enable confirmation that what happens actually is as it is;
- to provide a vehicle for re-engineering the processes to achieve the objectives of the project;

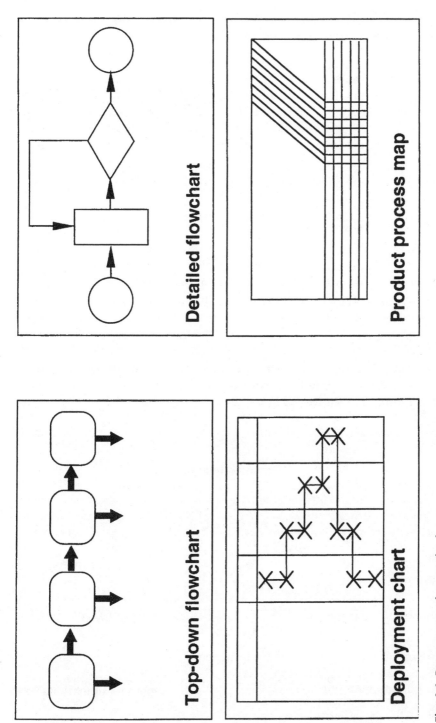

Top-down flowchart

Detailed flowchart

Deployment chart

Product process map

Fig. 4.1 Process mapping methods

- to allow discussion with senior management which leads to agreement to any recommended changes.

There are a number of approaches to describing processes, the majority of which can be collected under the generic term 'process modelling'. There are also many software tools available to support this modelling. Choosing the right methods and tools can be a headache for embarking on a BPR exercise. There is no 'best' approach for all BPR projects. The approach should be chosen to suit the communication and re-engineering objectives of the individual project.

Shown below are some examples of the approaches available.

HOW TO MANAGE YOUR BPR PROJECT

BPR in practice

There are a wide variety of approaches to 'doing' BPR. All share a common set of objectives, namely to build organisations which are customer focused, process-orientated and have appropriate structures and systems. In doing so, they also seek to reduce costs, improve quality, enhance service and speed up response times.

Changing a process involves people, systems and the process itself. The BPR project can therefore be viewed as combining these aspects in an integrated approach as shown in Figure 4.2.

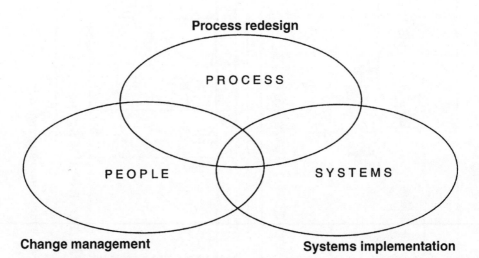

Fig. 4.2 The BPR project

The starting point of any BPR project must include the following:

- Senior management commitment – without this the cross-functional aspects of BPR will ensure that other managers stifle or inhibit the project.
- Creation of a 'Top Notch' BPR team – representatives of different areas of the organisation giving credibility to the project and its recommendations. Reasons for selecting team members frequently include:
  - project management skills
  - expertise in the processes
  - authority within the organisation
  - creative thinking ability
  - stakeholder in any change.
- Preparing the BPR plan of approach – the box below shows an approach which brings in the key components.

These phases can be described as set out in Figure 4.3.

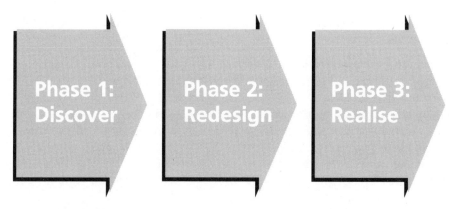

Fig. 4.3 Breakpoint BPR

Phase 1: Discover

The objectives of the **Discover** phase are to identify the business improvement opportunities and to secure buy-in for changes in processes. The key stages and activities within the phase will be to:

- **agree the scope** and objectives of the project;
- **identify and organise** the project team;
- **establish roles** and working arrangements;
- **train the team** members including key staff and explain the approach to be taken;
- **initial fact finding** through questionnaires, interviews, 'routing by

walking about' (walk through of sample processes) and suggestion schemes;

- **assess** the current high-level business processes and opportunities for improvement;
- **identify the targets for redesign;**
- **process mapping** which will provide a full end-to-end view of the processes;
- **value-added analysis** to identify in broad terms the high cost and low value activities.

During Phase 1 it is important to assess the willingness for change and identify risks and opportunities when processes are re-engineered. At the end of the **Discover** phase you need to have selected the appropriate processes on which to focus, and be clear on the current level of performance.

Phase 2: Redesign

The focus of the **Redesign** phase is on the specific processes for re-engineering identified in Phase 1. Key activities within this stage will be:

- **analyse best practice benchmarks** to assist the project team to gain an understanding of best practice and the processes and techniques which have delivered this;
- **generate ideas** using innovation workshop techniques to develop a view as to how the processes could be re-designed to maximise effectiveness and efficiency;
- **develop ideas** through mapping the 'to be' processes comparing cost structures, identifying preferred options for each process and testing with staff by walk through;
- **walk through of the key processes** to test out the understanding of the redesigned process.

The output from the **Redesign** phase is a set of preferred options including a case for action which outlines the broad savings and other benefits, together with the associated risks.

Phase 3: Realise

The final **Realise** phase comprises the development of the selected process options and implementation planning. The key steps are:

- **implement new processes** within an overall implementation plan. The priorities will be determined by impact on performance, implementation risk and benefits, as well as readiness for change;

- **monitor performance** against performance criteria established in the new processes and take corrective action as required. This will be a continuous activity which will check and monitor the success of the process redesign.

CHAPTER 5

Benchmarking

Knowledge shall be sought from all over the world and thus shall be strengthened the foundation of the imperial polity.

Emperor Meiji's Charter Oath – 1868

INTRODUCTION

When the Japanese decided to modernise their nation in the last century, so that they could stand up to the western imperial powers, they turned to one of the oldest management techniques in the world – benchmarking. Japanese were sent abroad to learn about the technology, the production methods, the financial and legal systems that were the underlying engines of European and American manufacturing, and then set about their introduction and application.

At the end of the 20th century it is the turn of European and American manufacturers to go to Japan and learn their techniques, technology and management methods. The classic example of this is Rank Xerox who benchmarked themselves against Canon, who were selling office machines for what it cost Rank Xerox to make them. The lessons Xerox learned from benchmarking are credited with being one of the main factors behind their revival in the 1980s.

The key to the turnaround in Japan in the 19th century, and of many UK private sector companies in the 1980s and 1990s, is that they were concerned with identifying best practice and applying it. They were not merely interested in measuring the performance gap. They sought to understand the underlying reasons for performance gaps and then close them through programmes of improvement.

The aim of this chapter is to describe the relevance of benchmarking to the public sector, the different approaches to its application, the main elements of a benchmarking project, and the problems and the technical skills needed to achieve best practice.

WHAT IS BENCHMARKING?

Benchmarking can be defined as the comparison of business practices and performance levels between organisations to gain new insights and to identify opportunities for making improvements in the economy, efficiency or effectiveness of an organisation's activities. In broad terms three main approaches, which are not mutually exclusive, can be identified.

Metrics

An approach which focuses on the calculation of numerical performance indicators such as unit costs, turnaround time, error rates. Many civil service executive agencies have formal targets set, based on such indicators. CIPFA statistics are produced to provide the raw data for metric-based benchmarks between local authorities.

Qualitative

This approach assesses an organisation against definitions of best practice. The analysis is largely qualitative and based on assessment against rigorous definitions of working practices and policies for a specified business practice. The approach is best summarised in 'innocence to excellence grids' as illustrated in Table 5.1. Such grids would be developed in increasing levels of detail process by process.

Process

This approach focuses on the comparison of the processes and activities underlying the performance of the function, e.g. finance, purchasing or customer service. It will map the activities undertaken and collect the resources consumed by those activities; it will also analyse the practices, working methods and policies that determine the performance of those activities. While the approach will collect metrics, its main thrust is to understand how performance can be improved.

These approaches are not mutually exclusive and their value depends on the purpose of the project. Figure 5.1 summarises the various approaches.

The most beneficial approach is one that seeks to identify how an organisation can improve and can secure returns to the investment of scarce resources that benchmarking will require. Performance surveys are a useful diagnostic tool and can provide targets to aim at but do not tell you what improvements can be made and how to implement them.

This is likely to require a combination of approaches. Real advantages of benchmarking, those that result in tangible improvements, are achieved

Table 5.1 Purchasing maturity profile – self-assessment form

Production Purchasing	Innocence	Awareness	Understanding	Competence	Excellence
Supply management	Many 'traditional' suppliers	Financial/QA suppliers vetting prior to approval	Commodity based sourcing drivers supplier profile	Supplier partnership programme	Suppliers used as a resource in their own right
In-bound logistics	Supplier deliveries to agreed terms and conditions of supplier. Price dominant, no TAC analysis	Supplier delivers to agreed terms and conditions of order. Price dominant. Some consolidation by EOQ	Supplier delivers by agreed times, lots and packaging. Analysis of TAC exposes price and logistics cost balance	Control of supplier process to JIT principles. Analysis of TAC and co-operation to reduce TAC	Suppliers integrated in total supply chain. Cost analysis of total supply chain
Planning requirements	No systems support. Suppliers driving replenishment	Stand-alone planning systems. Basic MRP utilised	Integrated MRP and materials management systems. Planning integrated with inventory management and driven by forecast	Integrated MRP and internal logistics. Integration of planning process from sales order to supplier	Integration of customer order recording and supply chain systems and process
Quality	Basic quality criteria established with suppliers	Quality criteria based on average quality levels expected	Quality management programme defining customers quality audit for suppliers	Quality management process based on supplier self-certification	Global supplier self-assessment and rating
Inventory management	Inventory managed to support continuous production process	Inventory managed to support continuous production process	Inventory managed to support JIT manufacturing, deliveries increased, loss reduced	Supply partnership drives inventory up the supply chain	Zero inventory in incoming stores and minimum in supplier inventory chain

Notes: EOQ – Economic Order Quantity; TAC – Total Acquisition Cost; MRP – Material Requirements Plan; JIT – Just In Time

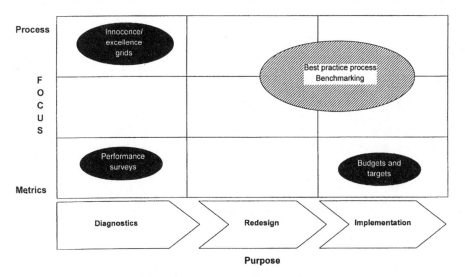

Fig. 5.1 How are companies approaching benchmarking?

when an organisation combines the collection of comparative performance metrics with the analysis and comparison of processes. The metrics bring problem areas to the attention of management, and the analysis of processes and best practice reveal ways to correct them.

In terms of comparators there is a natural progression from internal benchmarks to best in class.

Definitions of these comparators are:

- **internal** – comparisons are made betweeen separate divisions or departments of the same organisation where similiar processes are performed. This is particularly well suited to government departments with networked offices such as the Inland Revenue or the Department of Social Security;
- **direct competitors** – external comparisons are made with organisations providing the same product or service. This is particularly relevant for services facing market testing or compulsory competitive tendering;
- **other public sector bodies** – external comparisons are made with other bodies with the same control and legal environment and performing similar processes so that transaction based government departments such as the Land Registry and the Driver Vehicle Licensing Agency might compare analagous processes. The validity of comparison could be extended to overhead functions such as finance or purchasing;
- **best practice** – external comparisons with organisations in any sector but having similiar business processes. Therefore government departments with paper based, high volume transactions may look to the High Street

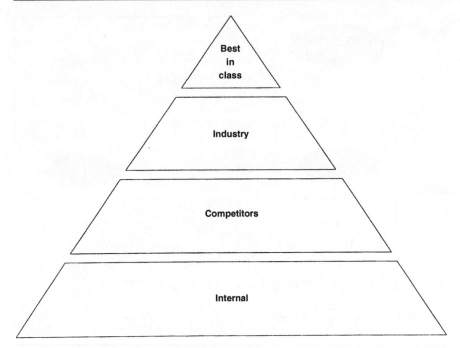

Fig. 5.2 Types of comparators used

financial service industry to learn how to handle casework. A Ministry of Defence repair workshop may look to Japanese car manufacturers to study their stock control methods.

Whilst some of the most profitable lessons and insights can be learned from organisations from different sectors, it is often helpful to start with internal benchmarking, comparing performance metrics between different offices or sites, understanding the processes and methods that explain differences in metrics and what is best internal practice before going outside. Internal data is easier to collect because there should be no problems of confidentiality, and its quality should be easier to maintain because it is easier to control common definitions and ensure like is being compared with like. Figure 5.3 illustrates the trade-offs to be made between the various comparators.

BENCHMARKING IN THE PRIVATE SECTOR

A survey into benchmarking in the private sector was conducted on behalf of Coopers & Lybrand and the Confederation of British Industries in 1994. Its findings showed how extensively it was used and the reasons for its increasing popularity as a management tool. More than two thirds of the UK's top

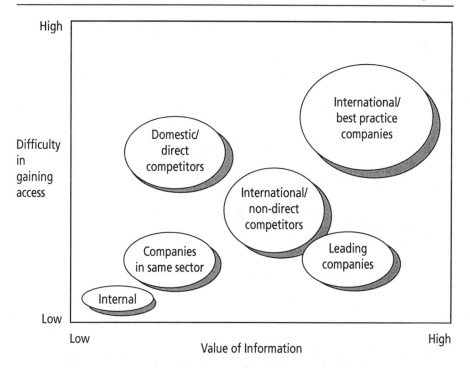

Fig. 5.3 **Trade-offs between different benchmarking partners**

1,000 companies use it to assess and improve their performance. Moreover, it is used in a wide number of different business functions. Figure 5.4 shows the functions where the private sector is using benchmarking.

Customer service, logistics, human resources, research and development, finance, purchasing and information services are all functions critical to the performance of public sector organisations.

The same benefits identified by the survey are achievable by the public sector and just as relevant. The benefits are summarised below.

Benefits of benchmarking – the private sector experience

- enables meaningful and realistic targets to be set   90%
- helps companies gain new insights   91%
- motivates staff by showing what is possible   84%
- provides early warning of competitive disadvantage   79%
- fosters step change and quantum leap improvements   58%
- promotes team work and cross-functional learning   58%

The survey reveals a considerable use and positive view of benchmarking by the private sector, but are the same benefits relevant to the public sector?

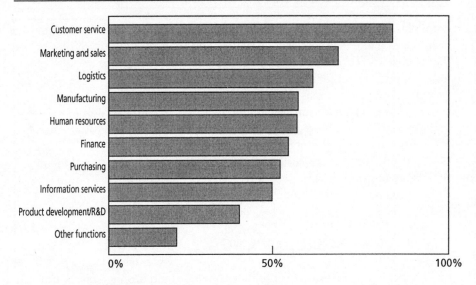

Fig. 5.4 Which functions use benchmarking?

WHAT CAN BENCHMARKING OFFER THE PUBLIC SECTOR?

The public sector has different pressures to the private sector but has the same needs to manage costs and service quality with increasing sophistication and continuous improvement. The scale of public sector reform in recent years is generating these pressures and has been extensive and continuous.

Pressures on the public sector

- funding reductions, e.g. Public Expenditure Surveys (PES) running cost freezes, caps on Council Tax rates, pay increases unfunded;
- internal markets, e.g. National Health Service, hard charging in government departments, growth in trading fund status;
- efficiency plans from government departments (introduced with the White Paper *Continuity and Change*);
- competing for quality programmes, i.e. market testing;
- compulsory competitive tendering;
- privatisation;
- next step agencies;
- Citizen's Charter commitments.

These reforms mean that the public sector has to justify continuing in-house provision of services, compete with the private sector and with itself, demonstrate year-on-year efficiency improvements, account for the quality of its service to customers and taxpayers and manage within funding levels that at best keep up with inflation but represent real decreases because of the 'relative price effect' of public sector resources.

The private sector has found that benchmarking is one technique to achieve the continuous improvement required to remain competitive in a global economy and the public sector should find it equally useful to manage the continuous improvement demanded by the pressures described above. More output for the same or less resource is something that many organisations have faced in the last decade.

Benchmarking can point the way but what does it entail?

THE PROCESS OF BENCHMARKING

Benchmarking studies can be undertaken as stand-alone projects but are more generally performed as part of major programmes of performance improvement such as business process re-engineering in which it forms an essential and complementary technique alongside the others described in this book. Its role in this respect is summarised in Figure 5.5.

The process of benchmarking is illustrated in Figure 5.6. This is not the only approach possible but it is one which the authors have used in many

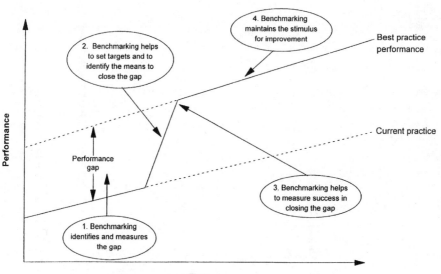

Fig. 5.5 Using benchmarking to improve performance

Benchmarking

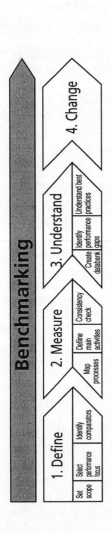

1. Define		2. Measure			3. Understand			4. Change
Set scope	Identify comparators	Map processes	Define main activities	Consistency check	Create performance databank	Identify performance gaps	Understand best practices	
	Select performance focus							

Areas of focus

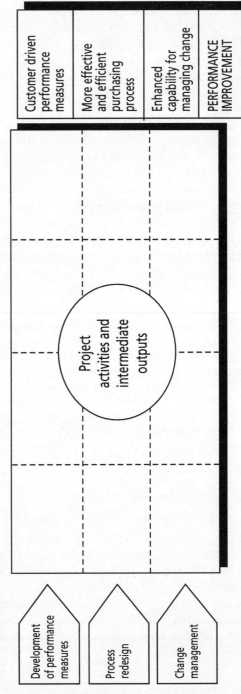

Project activities and intermediate outputs

- Development of performance measures
- Process redesign
- Change management

- Customer driven performance measures
- More effective and efficient purchasing process
- Enhanced capability for managing change
- PERFORMANCE IMPROVEMENT

Fig. 5.6 The approach to benchmarking

Process benchmarking is a four-staged approach each with defined tasks, activities and outputs

significant benchmarking projects and which is most likely to lead to real insights capable of practical implementation.

The approach seeks to incorporate the principles critical to the successful implementation of benchmarking.

Benchmarking – keys to success

- **Define the objectives of the project**
  Is it cost reduction, quality improvement or some other objective? The answer will determine choice of processes and the definition of comparators and set expectations of the benefits being sought.
- **Focus on processes and the underlying methods and policies**
  It is the comparison of these with your benchmarks that will lead to practical improvement opportunities.
- **Select the right organisations to benchmark against**
  You will not learn unless you benchmark against the best.
- **Get independent assessment of your current performance and operations**
  It is easy for organisations to deceive themselves about the reasons for performance gaps and to stress how unique their operations are.
- **Be open**
  If you expect to obtain detailed, possibly sensitive, data about other organisations then you have to be prepared to give something back.
- **Prioritise the functions to be benchmarked**
  Successful benchmarking can be a time-consuming process. Time spent on it should be focused on those processes critical to your performance as an organisation.

A benchmarking project is likely to consist of four main stages.

1. Prepare

In this stage the main tasks might include:

- defining the scope and objectives of the study
- defining the breadth and detail of the processes to be analysed and the type of comparators or metrics to be developed
- deciding on the use of any software to be used for recording and analysing the data collected, e.g. for mapping processes
- design of any data analysis forms and questionnaires
- identifying possible partners to benchmark against
- training the team in benchmarking and associated techniques and their roles and responsibilities

2. Collect

In this stage the main tasks would be:

- gathering data internally on processes and related metrics
- recruiting external partners
- collecting external data
- refining the data to ensure it is consistent in definition and coverage

3. Analyse

In this stage the main tasks would be:

- collate the process and metric data into a single set of process and data benchmarks
- compare and contrast internal and external findings (see illustrative Figure 5.7)
- draw up best practice models for each process (see Table 5.1)
- highlight improvement opportunities

4. Change

In this stage the main tasks would be:

- develop specific projects and plans to investigate the identified opportunities
- build consensus to the changes proposed, and implement

Not all projects follow this 'ideal' structure and flexibility is essential as illustrated in the case study below.

Case Study – Turning round a local authority Direct Labour Organisation

A particular assignment we were involved with illustrates the approach and principles described above. The client was a local authority Direct Labour Organisation that was required to make a 5 per cent return on its capital employed, but was in fact making a substantial loss. There was a danger that the DLO could be closed down by the Secretary of State for the Environment; a quick turn-around of its operational efficiency and profitability was needed.

The first step was to analyse the efficiency of its main activities from internal accounting documents and derive key performance indicators for comparison against other DLOs and private sector competitors. It became clear from the performance metrics and accounting analyses that it was one particular function and its processes where the severest performance gaps lay.

Attention was directed to these processes and they were analysed in detail

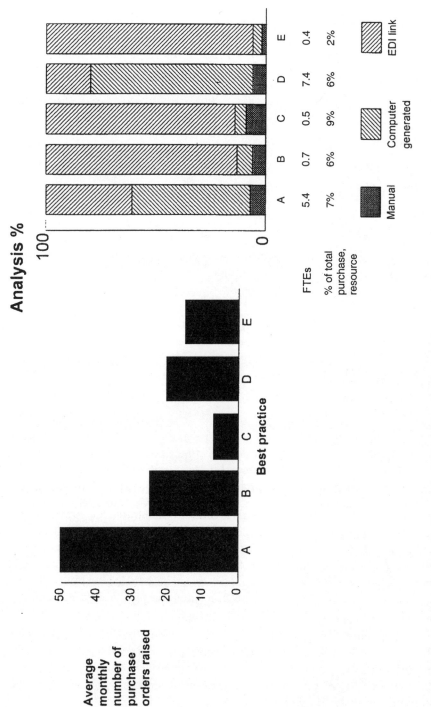

Fig. 5.7 Purchasing process activities – numbers and graphical analysis compared with best practice

using activity mapping techniques such as 'routing by walking about'. This involved taking a core process such as fulfilling a customer order and following it through the organisation from receipt to completion of the service. The process was compared with best practice developed from data created from previous jobs in DLOs.

Comparison with similiar private sector companies in the same industry was not appropriate because they were direct competitors for the same market. However market prices were obtained for the services and these set a benchmark to aim at; the DLO knew that its costs had to be low enough to fall within the market price benchmark and to leave sufficient surplus to make its profit target.

The comparative analysis revealed significant opportunities for improvement such as introducing mobile van stocks, using mobile telephones to send details of jobs (rather than returning to depot), pre-bagging of materials to complete standard jobs, introducing multi-skill working. Some of these improvements were 'quick wins' and produced immediate results; at the end of the financial year a 30 per cent loss was transformed to break-even. Some of the improvements required long-term investment, for example to develop systems to monitor plant and vehicle utilisation and to produce detailed cost and profitability reports. All of the improvements required considerable culture change to embed new working practices and to focus attention on customers and internal efficiency.

PROBLEMS WITH BENCHMARKING

Benchmarking has much to offer the public sector in coping with the many pressures that it faces. However, there are many problems that need to be overcome if its benefits are to be realised fully. The main problems are as follows.

Comparability of data

When comparing performance between organisations it is essential to ensure that like is compared with like, that common definitions of metrics and processes are used and that the comparators are performing similiar processes within similiar constraints. This is why it is so important to ensure the right comparators are selected and that data collected is consistent. One of the problems with CIPFA's local authority statistics is that consistent definitions of costing and service are hard to enforce, while the particular situation of individual authorities will affect their apparent performance.

Level of detail

Excessive detail in the collection of metrics and the mapping of processes can divert effort from the more value-adding features of benchmarking which should be the identification of best practice and implementing the lessons that it teaches. Benchmarking is an art more than a science; the metrics are collected to point out areas of concern and high achievement and are a means to focus effort where it will bring the greatest reward.

Scope

Linked to the problems with excessive levels of detail is the need to restrict the scope of any single benchmarking exercise. Best practice benchmarking is a resource intensive technique and projects are more successful where the scope is restricted to a few processes. This is why it is a crucial task of the initial phase of the project or for a more general performance initiative to define the objectives and to prioritise areas for investigation.

Confidentiality of data

The identification of best practice data from external comparators could require confidential data, especially if it is to be useful. Organisations operating in a highly competitive environment or who could attract the attention of the public expenditure control divisions of the Treasury may be wary of publishing their sensitive data. Benchmarking clubs are increasingly popular

because they offer the opportunities to provide sensitive data to a common point where it is collected, structured on a common basis and presented anonymously for the club members. Such clubs require the services of an honest broker to manage them and management consultancies frequently play this role.

CONCLUSION

The evidence of the private sector points to the usefulness of benchmarking in managing the conflicting pressures of cost reduction and rising expectations of improved service levels.

Public sector organisations face a type of benchmarking in the form of market testing and compulsory competitive tendering and internal markets. In coming to terms with these initiatives the public sector is forced into benchmarking if it is to prepare in-house operations adequately. Benchmarking is not a substitute for market testing but it is an excellent preparatory tool to ensure that best value for money is obtained from the exercise.

It is not a panacea that can resolve all performance management issues and it can be resource intensive. This is why the best value from benchmarking is usually obtained when it is used as part of a more general improvement programme. A business process re-engineering programme for example will cover many of the activities in a purely benchmarking project; they will be defining problem areas, mapping and costing current processes, looking at opportunities for improvement and setting targets. It is really best seen as one weapon in an armoury of techniques.

CHAPTER 6

Activity based management

INTRODUCTION

The subject of this chapter is often misunderstood and much of the uncertainty has been caused by practitioners with little or no knowledge of the subject and even less experience. The reason for this general lack of knowledge is that the public sector has, until recently, been the forgotten sector in terms of performance improvement initiatives. However, with the advent of internal markets and consumer choice the section is now looking towards introducing commercial awareness and commercial styles of management. This had led to a change of focus away from internal requirements and onto customer requirements and increasing profitability.

ACTIVITY BASED MANAGEMENT (ABM) – DEFINITIONS

Activity based management (ABM) is the management and control of enterprise performance using activity based information as a primary means of decision support.

This appears to be all embracing, but true ABM involves the use of 'activities' in planning, budgeting, costing, modelling and performance measurement. It is therefore of fundamental importance for organisations to have a clear vision of how they want their ABM system to look and to define the information that such a system should deliver.

ABM is not BPR. ABM is an ongoing process whereas BPR is generally one-off; ABM is organisation-wide whereas BPR concentrates on core business processes. However, as we shall see, ABM and other performance improvement initiatives are linked closely.

It is important to dispel all misunderstanding at an early stage. One of the biggest problems with ABM is that nearly everyone has a different interpretation of exactly what ABM is, and even more problematical is the fact that the terms and the terminology used differ widely.

There are some fundamental definitions required in order to assimilate even the most basic knowledge of ABM:

- **business process** – a sequence of related and inter dependent activities that combine to achieve a specific output;
- **activity** – a 'process' of using resources to convert inputs into an output, e.g. process a passport application;
- **input** – the factors other than resources required to perform the activity, e.g. a written request or a purchase order;
- **supplier** – the external or internal provider of the input;
- **output** – the product of an activity. It is what internal or external customers receive, e.g. a driving licence;
- **customer** – the recipient of the output of the activity (the next person in the business process);
- **cost driver** – the root cause or reason for the activity to occur;
- **output measure** – a quantifiable (volumetric) measure of the output of an activity, e.g. number of applications handled;
- **performance measure** – a measure of how well the activity was performed in terms of cost, quality or time.

INTRODUCTION TO ABM

ABM is fundamentally different to the way in which organisations manage today. In fact the traditional way in which some organisations manage can actually hinder performance improvement.

Consider the following common public sector practices.

Budgeting by cost element

Problem: work is not visible. All cost centre statements appear similar – only the numbers against the cost types change. For example, every cost centre will have the following cost types in its budget – staff costs, local purchase, communications, information technology, travel and subsistence, etc. However an 'outsider' cannot see what the cost centre actually does! Vote accounting only exacerbates this problem. Resource accounting will require managers to account for **all** of their resources. This means that budget should be devolved to the lowest possible level of responsibility.

Functional organisation

Problem: there is optimisation within individual departments, internal competition and little or no cross-functional co-ordination. There is also no obvious relationship between what the departments do and the final customer's requirement. Imagine a hospital attempting to arrange an operation but failing to book an anaesthetist. The customer wants the final service, i.e. the completed operation – they are not interested in the functional peculiarities of the hospital's organisation structure. A cross-functional approach helps to alleviate such problems.

Incremental budgeting

Problem: wasteful activities are hidden (see chapter on PBB). Managers assume that activities performed during previous years are all adding value to the department – this is fundamentally incorrect. Budgeting should involve a review of **all** a department's activities.

Hierarchical organisations

Problem: improvement is seen as management's responsibility. Staff do not feel empowered to make decisions and communication channels are long and complex. Management should be regarded as a control mechanism and if processes are under control there should be minimal requirement for ongoing management. Hierarchical management structures lead to long lead times mainly due to the intense bureaucracy associated with such structures. Consider the preparation of a policy statement. How many drafts and re-drafts are there? How many levels of approval exist?

After-the-event reporting

Problem: variances are not prevented and by the time that they are reported it is often too late to take corrective action. In many public sector departments there is an abundance of data but very little information. Managers are generally unaware that there is a problem until it is too late to take corrective action.

Fixed and variable costs are separated

Problem: a 'fixed' cost is a cost we cannot change therefore we shall ignore it! We must move towards the concept of used and unused capacity. For example, do not apportion all your property costs across all departments. You should identify how much space you really need and identify the rest as excess capacity. [In a market testing environment your competitors would not build wasteful costs into their bid – so why should you!] Unfortunately, public sector budgets are often cash based and do not take into account non-cash costs such as depreciation.

Improvement is the responsibility of the senior management

Problem: no one else in the organisation 'signs up' to the improvement initiative. Managers feel bitter; staff lose commitment and the improvement initiative fails.

PREREQUISITES FOR ABM

ABM has evolved to alleviate many of the above problems but in order to succeed there are several prerequisites:

- the organisation must have the capacity to change. Do not attempt to introduce too many changes at any one time;
- there must be sufficient pressure to change. These pressures include cost reduction targets in PES, market testing, customer service targets (e.g. Citizen's Charter), formal performance targets, etc.;
- there must be senior management commitment. Many projects fail due to a lack of direction from the top. ABM needs input from across the entire organisation. If senior management commitment is absent then **you will fail**;
- there should be a well documented plan. All participants should be aware of the vision for ABM and know what they are doing and **why** they are doing it.

PRINCIPLES OF ABM

The main concept of ABM is that:

People do activities and activities consume resources.

Therefore controlling your activities automatically controls the resources required.

There are seven core principles of ABM:

- **manage activities not resources** – understanding why you do activities and their associated costs provides new insights into your cost base;
- **let customers drive activities** – activities should be aligned to the needs of your internal or external customers. Who are your customers? Would they pay for the service you provide?
- **streamline activities within business processes** – understand how the activities within your organisation inter-relate;
- **eliminate wasteful activities** – do not do activities that could be eliminated without detriment to your final product or service. Eliminate bureaucracy;

"We're here to eliminate bureaucracy "

- **improve activities continuously** – link ABM into any Total Quality programme. Ensure that you incorporate procedures that encourage continuous improvement. Remember, your competitors will be looking to win all invitations to tender;
- **do activities right continuously** – costs are incurred every time an activity is done differently (or incorrectly). A one-off request is far more costly to undertake/process than a common request. Minimise variation;
- **flex capacity to activity workload** – do not burden yourself with unnecessary costs. Understand how much resource you really need. Be innovative when managing peaks and troughs – for example use sub-contract staff or introduce shifts.

ABM provides new insights into departmental costs

Figure 6.1 begins to lift the veil of ABM. Imagine having to manage a cost base like the one on the left. Human nature would lead you to reducing the high value items (such as salaries and wages) but what effect would this have on your activities and customers? The view on the right tells a completely different story. It is now evident how the budget is spent – this information can be used in a variety of ways such as 'a stick to beat people with' or a 'shield to deflect criticism'! These are extreme uses but it is now obvious how much information could be used to improve the management of an organisation.

Figure 6.1 illustrates the concept of 'activity costing' not 'activity based costing (ABC)' while Table 6.1 takes the concept a stage further by identify-

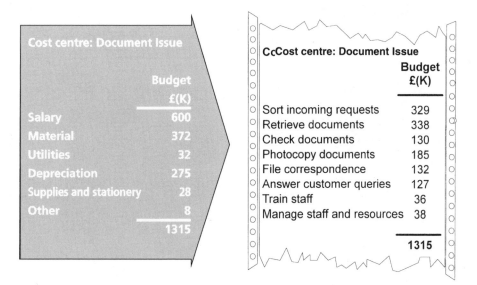

Fig. 6.1 Activity costing – an example

ing output measures and volumes for each activity. This output measure can be used to plan activity workload, set objectives and to measure the effectiveness of a department. The cost per unit of output is obtained by dividing the total activity cost by the number of outputs.

Table 6.1 Activity costing – output measures

Activities	Cost (£)	Output measures	Volume of output (number)	Cost/unit of output (£)
Produce purchase orders	50,000	purchase orders	15,000	3.33
Pay invoices	40,000	invoices	10,000	4.00
Vet suppliers	20,000	suppliers	1,000	20.00
Process expense claims	25,000	claims	5,000	5.00
Handle queries on expenses	30,000	queries	2,000	15.00
Produce monthly management accounts	75,000	monthly reports	12	6250.00
Produce quarterly expenditure returns	25,000	expenditure returns	4	6250.00
Produce appropriation accounts	25,000	subheads	30	833.00
Produce parliamentary estimates	30,000	subheads	30	1000.00

THE ABM APPROACH

The ABM approach can be broken down into several steps:

- planning;
- education and awareness;
- business process/activity definition;
- data collection (activity analysis);
- performance improvement techniques;
- planning the ongoing system;
- implementation.

Each stage may be done with different levels of detail and some can be omitted completely. The number of steps and the level of detail will be determined by two main factors – the objectives of the study and the 'vision' of the ABM system.

Planning

The planning phase of an ABM project is key. ABM is essentially a participative process and while elements can be done in isolation this is not the recommended route. The planning phase should include:

- a project plan with key activities/milestones/dates;
- a project management structure;
- a list of the aims and objectives of the study;
- the scope of the study;
- the roles and responsibilities of all those involved;
- a change management strategy/plan.

Education and awareness

ABM is company-wide and requires significant investment in training and education. The amount of training depends on the coverage and objectives. For example, if ABM is used to develop an in-house market testing bid, it is possible to train only those who are involved in constructing the bid. However, if the aim is to inject some commercialism into the organisation then far greater coverage is required. If ABM is to be used for resource accounting or efficiency planning purposes then it **may** be sufficient to train only those managers likely to be involved.

Remember ABM is not 'something done by an accountant tucked away on the 7th floor of an office block'.

Business process/activity definition

Business process and activity definitions are the core building block of the ABM methodology. This phase begins to induce new ways of thinking into organisations since it makes wide use of 'management workshops'. The aim is to get a group of knowledgeable people to define the core business processes.

A core business process has several characteristics. It must:

- be felt or valued by the customer;
- create an opportunity for differentiation or competitive advantage;
- be indifferent to organisation structure;
- be critical to organisation success;
- be focused on delivering a result, not on monitoring other core processes.

Once the core processes have been defined it is possible to identify the activities. There are two ways to do this:

- define the activities within each department/function and then link them to the business processes (bottom-up); or
- decompose the business processes using a top-down process mapping tool. The exact level of decomposition depends on the nature of the work (see Figure 6.2).

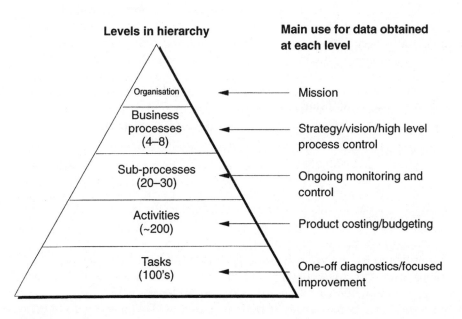

Fig. 6.2

For the majority of ABM applications (including market testing, activity based costing and management information systems) it is generally not necessary to go to more than two levels of decomposition. A simple rule of thumb is 6–10 activities per department.

There are also some basic rules to observe when defining activities:

- activities generally need to represent a significant level of expenditure;
- activities should be written in the form of 'verb' + 'noun', e.g. process order or answer query;
- activities (or at least primary activities) should have a measurable output.

In order to eliminate duplication and ambiguity it is advisable to set up an activity dictionary. An activity dictionary is simply a listing of activities by function with their associated definitions and outputs. (It is possible to build on this data and include reference to the business processes and some kind of activity classification, e.g. primary/secondary but this is not always necessary.)

Data collection (activity analysis)

The data collection phase is probably the single most time-consuming phase but it can be shortened considerably with good planning and the use of Information Technology.

The data collection phase is initially undertaken in a 'one-off' environment since organisations like to develop the methodology prior to investing in large IT projects. This means that there is generally a large amount of 'unravelling' of budgets to be done. Data collection entails tracing **all** costs within the organisation to the departments in which the activities are performed. The first problem in the public sector is identifying the complete cost base. Imagine attempting to do comparative benchmarking without knowing how much IT or space you require! The only way to do this exercise effectively is to decide at the outset where the costs lie, and then to trace these costs to the user departments based upon some 'fair' means. For example:

- space is often traced by area occupied;
- IT can be traced by either amount of processing time or number of terminals.

Remember, ABM involves tracing all costs within the business to the activities that consume those costs.

Once costs have been traced to the departments, the next stage is to trace these costs to the activities that are performed within the departments. On one-off exercises this is best done using manager's estimates but ongoing systems require links to be made to ledgers/feeder systems.

The first step is to trace **staff costs** to activities. This may be done using timesheeting (if data is available) or manager's estimates. Once this has been done, the **non-staff costs** such as travel and consumables need to be traced to the activities that consume them.

The aim of this step is to assign all of the department's costs to the activities that are performed within the department (see Table 6.2). This is also the approach used in activity based budgeting. In budgeting exercises it may be sufficient to use 'average costs'. For example if a department is using a range of vehicles and the average cost of hire is £50 per day then a budget could be constructed using the average daily rate multiplied by the predicted daily usage.

Table 6.2 Activity analysis – departmental costs

Department: Data Security	Labour (£K)	Depreciation (£K)	Travel (£K)	Supplies (£K)	Facilities (£K)	Total (£K)
Develop new business	25.0			1.0	1.5	27.5
Maintain database	57.5	100.0		2.3	3.5	163.3
Rectify errors	25.0			1.0	1.5	27.5
Draft reports	67.5			2.7	4.1	74.3
Deal with special requests	50.0			2.0	3.0	55.0
Plan workload	67.5			2.7	4.1	74.3
Prepare policy statements	25.0			1.0	1.5	27.5
Visit suppliers	42.5		20.0	1.7	2.5	66.7
Administer branch	80.0			3.2	4.7	87.9
Training	10.0		30.0	0.4	0.6	41.0
Other	50.0			2.0	3.0	55.0
Total costs	500.0	100.0	50.0	20.0	30.0	700.0

Performance improvement techniques

The old school of 'activity based costing' enthusiasts often failed to capitalise on the full range of techniques described here. They were frequently satisfied with knowing how much their final products or services cost and made informed strategic decisions based upon these results. However, the more advanced organisations began to use their activity database to make inroads into their cost base.

A range of performance improvement techniques have evolved which can be used either on a 'one-off' or continuous improvement basis:

- cost driver analysis;
- activity classification;
- activity based costing;
- performance measurement.

Cost driver analysis

A cost driver is the root cause, or reason, for activities to occur. Improvement initiatives should be focused on the cost driver. Common cost drivers in the public sector include:

- organisation policy;
- bureaucratic procedures;
- inappropriate layout of building;
- lack of training;
- poor planning.

The identification of cost drivers is best achieved by:

- assembling a group of people familiar with the business process;
- using problem solving techniques to determine the main cost drivers, e.g. brainstorming or 'cause and effect' (fishbone diagrams).

Activity classification

This is one of the most powerful performance improvement tools used within the ABM framework. It can be used to deliver one-off benefits as well as in an ongoing system.

There are many ways to classify activities but for them to be successful there are a number of criteria to observe:

- classification must be viewed as a tool to assist with cost reduction/performance improvement;
- all those involved with classifying activities should be comfortable with applying the classification definitions (such as primary/secondary) or value-added/non-value-added);
- the numerical values obtained through such an exercise are indications of the potential for improvement – activity classification is subjective – it is not a precise science!

The two most common ways of classifying activities are primary/secondary and value-added/non-value-added (VA/NVA).

- **primary** – contribute directly to the mission or objective of a department or process. The output is used outside the organisation or by another department within the organisation;
- **secondary** – support the primary activities. For example, monitor budgets, attend training, manage staff;
- **value-added** – essential to the product or service received by the customer and necessary for the organisation to remain an ongoing concern;
- **non-value-added** – could be eliminated without detriment to the final

product or service. For example if the activity was done right first time, customer requirements were properly understood or the process was designed efficiently.

Through a series of questions we can determine if an activity adds value:

- could the activity be eliminated if some prior activity were done differently or correctly?
- does the technology exist to eliminate the activity?
- could the activity be eliminated without impacting the form fit or function of our customer service?
- is the activity required by an external customer and will the customer pay for it?

To summarise the above criteria consider Figure 6.3. This demonstrates how we should treat the activities once they have been classified. Primary value-added activities are the main reason for the organisation to exist. They should be improved and then continuously improved. Secondary value-added activities only exist by virtue of there being primary activities. They should therefore be simplified and reduced to a minimum level. They are, in

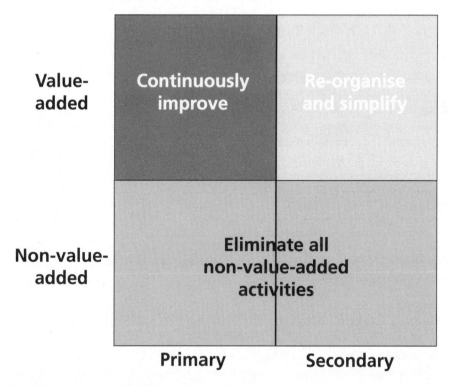

Fig. 6.3 Classifying activities

effect, 'enabling' activities. NVA (whether primary or secondary) should, in the long term, be eliminated.

Activity based costing (ABC)

ABC is the seed from which ABM has grown. The exact mechanisms are now well established and so only a brief overview is presented here. The principle of ABC is to trace costs to activities and then on to 'cost objects'. Cost objects can be products, services, projects, customers etc. ABC is the method by which many government departments are seeking to introduce the concept of 'output costing'. In this context the word output is synonymous with cost object – hence the confusion.

Figure 6.4 illustrates an overview of the ABC methodology. There are subtle variations on this theme but they are all very similar.

The secret of success with ABC is not to create too many activities. There has been a tendency to decompose processes to the nth degree. It is necessary to ask a number of questions before going into large amounts of detail:

• how are we going to collect this data on an ongoing basis?
• who is going to use this data?
• will more detail provide me with more accurate product/service costs?
• do we need to measure the performance of these activities?

The prime benefits of introducing ABC into the public sector are:

• service costs can be defined accurately;
• activities become visible;
• there is a focus on outputs (cost objects);
• true costs are identified;
• managers can compare the relative strategic importance of particular activities in the organisation with the level of resources consumed by them.

Activity based performance measurement

This is the area where most of the improvement approaches come together. The principles of activity based performance measures are well understood. Activity based performance measures should:

• act as motivators;
• be challenging (but achievable);
• be aligned to business and customer goals;
• be visible;
• be easy to collect.

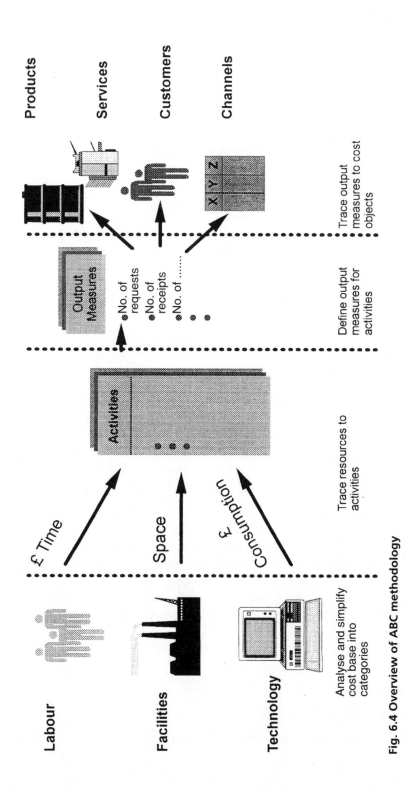

Fig. 6.4 Overview of ABC methodology

Figure 6.5 illustrates the hierarchy of performance measures. Remember that if processes are under control then they need only be measured at strategic control points. **Do not measure the organisation to death!**

When acting upon the information provided by performance measures one should adopt the 'balanced scorecard' approach. That is, balance the targets you are trying to achieve (such as quality, time and service targets) with the cost and systems associated with achieving these targets.

Planning the ongoing system

This is where the 'fun' starts. An ongoing ABM system is a highly sought after prize. The army are probably as far down this route as anyone. They are attempting to cost their activities, objectives and outputs and link these to their overall performance measurement system. The aim is to be able to do benchmarking between similar units, plan at an activity level, report costs by activity and army output (cost object) and to model different scenarios.

The ongoing system requires a major study into the present and future information requirements of the organisation. It is possible to build a theoretical framework (see Figure 6.6) but unless organisations are aware of the full potential of such a system a good 'vision' is unlikely to materialise. One of the main barriers to developing a good ongoing system is that when managers are asked their requirements for an ABM system the most common response is 'What's ABM?'. This just reinforces the importance of education and awareness.

There are two main approaches to developing ongoing systems.

- standard packages;
- bespoke systems.

Provided that you do not want to tread into too much uncharted water there is a good selection of standard packages that can assist with a significant element of the ABM approach. For instance, the tracing of costs to activities and then on to cost objects, activity classification and linking activities on to business processes is well within the capability of the better packages. These packages also have links to feeder systems (such as general ledgers). The difficulties arise when you wish to tap into time management systems or performance measurement systems. Once you decide on the 'all singing, all dancing' approach you need to think about a bespoke solution.

Implementation

Implementation (or biting the bullet) can be broken down into two areas:

- **implementing the result of the performance improvement work** – some of

LEVEL OF MEASUREMENT

Company-wide
e.g. Licensing company

Business processes
e.g. Process licence applications

Departmental
e.g. Document replacement

Activity
e.g. Input documents

EXAMPLE MEASURES

- Average lead time
- Number of customer complaints
- Staff per licence processed

- Cost of process
- Error rates

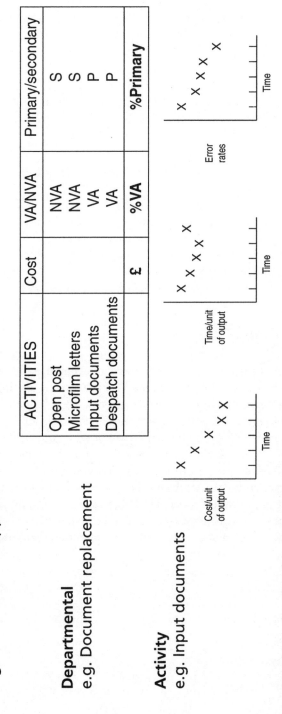

ACTIVITIES	Cost	VA/NVA	Primary/secondary
Open post		NVA	S
Microfilm letters		NVA	S
Input documents		VA	P
Despatch documents		VA	P
	£	**%VA**	**%Primary**

Fig. 6.5 A hierarchy of performance measures

the changes will be straightforward to implement (for example eliminating duplication, delays in layers of management). Others will require major implementation projects (such as introducing new computer systems or closing buildings). It is essential to define 'owners' for each change and to define a detailed implementation plan for each change;

- **managing the change** – this topic is covered in detail elsewhere so for brevity it will suffice to say, 'Don't forget to consider the people issues'. There will be winners and losers. Look for the 'win–win' solutions.

Links to other performance improvement initiatives

ABM can be introduced at any time. It can be used to:

- build on a **Total Quality** programme;
- provide useful data for **benchmarking**;
- provide a reference point from which to measure improvement *before* a **BPR** exercise; or
- provide ongoing management information *after* a **BPR** exercise.

THE WAY FORWARD

The future of ABM is still unclear. Many organisations still like to engage in the one-off exercise and reap the benefits of quick returns. Some install ABM systems and are satisfied with the knowledge that they know how much things really cost. Others implement activity/process based performance measures and remain happy knowing that their processes are in control. However, to obtain the step change in benefits from ABM it is necessary to invest significant time in training and systems technology. The aim must be to have all the information required to manage and improve the effectiveness of the organisation at the fingertips of the manager. A vision for the future may be depicted as shown in Figure 6.6. Here we can see the activity at the centre of an activity based management information system.

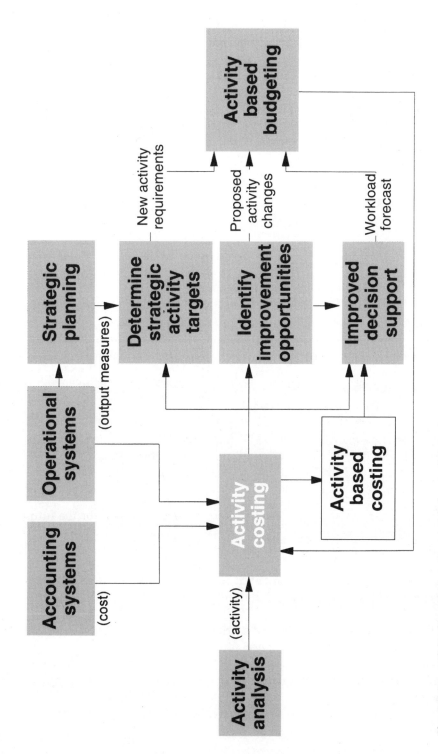

Fig. 6.6 An activity based management information system

CHAPTER 7

Priority based budgeting (PBB)

WHAT IS PBB? – A DEFINITION

Priority based budgeting is not the new flavour of the month, it has been around for many years. In the world of performance improvement methodologies, it is the packhorse that can be relied upon to do a good job.

PBB is a structured and highly participative approach to performance improvement that delivers both hard and soft benefits to an organisation; hard benefits being the more quantifiable changes often with a pound sign attached, soft benefits being less quantifiable and often relating to people and how they feel. The hard benefits can typically include cost reduction, planning, budgeting, improvement in services delivered, and the reallocation of resources from low to high priority areas.

The soft benefits can typically include greater understanding by staff of the business environment; improved skills in planning and budgeting; a clearer picture of how they fit into the overall direction of the organisation; better communication and understanding across functional groups; an increased understanding by budget holders of roles and responsibilities; ownership of plans and commitment to achieve target improvements; and greater assurance that plans are soundly based on the organisation's strategy and skills gained in planning and cost management.

The PBB programme:

- is undertaken by the manager of each budget with direction from top management. This then combines 'bottom-up' effort with 'top-down' direction and review;
- is thorough and detailed; it's hard work;
- is participative, everyone becomes involved;
- is catching, it develops a momentum of its own like the proverbial snowball – generally, by the end, nearly everyone becomes swept along even if they resist at first;
- is cost centre focused – it broadly accepts the existing organisational structure;

- is typically a one-off performance improvement programme, although it can be used annually, in particular if it is being used to set the budgets.

PBB has been described as 'an HR methodology with teeth'. It has the gift of combining a rigorous, highly structured approach that, we can say with the confidence born from many years of experience, can deliver the financial savings – this pleases the chief executive and the finance director, **plus** it is a methodology that is built upon an understanding of people, what motivates or de-motivates them and how one can enthuse large numbers of people and pull together their ideas.

Central to PBB is the clear distinction made between efficiency and effectiveness. It is important to look at whether a service is effective, i.e. if it achieves what the customer wants and then to look at ways to produce it efficiently i.e. with the minimum resources (staff or non-staff resources). It is deciding **what** to produce first and then **how** the service should be produced, which leads to doing the right things right.

WHY MIGHT YOU ADOPT PBB, AS OPPOSED TO ANOTHER METHODOLOGY?

A PBB programme offers the best approach to meet the performance improvement objectives if the right environment is in place both externally and internally.

The external environment – can you identify with this?

Imagine looking through the window of your organisation and describing what you see. Do you see a slightly threatening tangle of:

- government performance targets, reforms and reviews?
- reduced funding or threat of it?
- increased competition?
- whisperings of a threat of closure?
- possibility of being contracted out?

The internal environment – can you identify with this?

Turning back from the window and looking down the corridor of your organisation do you see:

- various performance improvement initiatives that have taken place but which appear unco-ordinated and have really only nibbled at the edges or dealt with the easy bits?

- contention existing within and between functions and cliques?
- contention existing on the level of service and which service the organisation should be providing?
- strong pressure groups such as unions that would have to see a fair system before any change could be made?

However, on the more positive side, do you also see:

- a fairly clear organisation where improving functions is preferable to a more radical and complex streamlining of business processes and reorganisation;
- a need for mechanisms to control the degree of radicalism of any improvement programme;
- lots of good ideas floating about the organisation, but the need for strong encouragement and a structure to help these ideas come down to earth and take root;
- junior and middle managers of at least average to good competency and certainly off the bottom rung;
- an appropriate sized organisation, i.e. cost base of perhaps £5 million or more.

WHY MIGHT YOU NOT ADOPT PBB?

Consider:
- do you really need to change? If it works, don't fix it;
- are there easier ways, for example extra funding or income?
- do you need to be more radical, for example ignore the existing organisational structure and reorganise first? Don't strengthen the wrong structure;
- do you need to sort out what your customer's needs are first? Don't provide the wrong services more efficiently;
- have you time; how near the door is the wolf? The financial benefits from PBB might take three months to start flowing and probably six to nine months to peak;
- do you need to determine your vision, strategic plan, or mission statement first? Don't move into top gear if you don't know where you are going, it might hurt.

In general, you should adopt the PBB approach if you have a significant cost reduction target. In the majority of cases the need to reduce costs in a way that is acceptable to the majority of staff is the first priority. The second is if you feel you have, broadly speaking, the right organisational structure which you want to stick with. You are generally aware of your customer requirements but need to deliver those services in the right way and at the right cost.

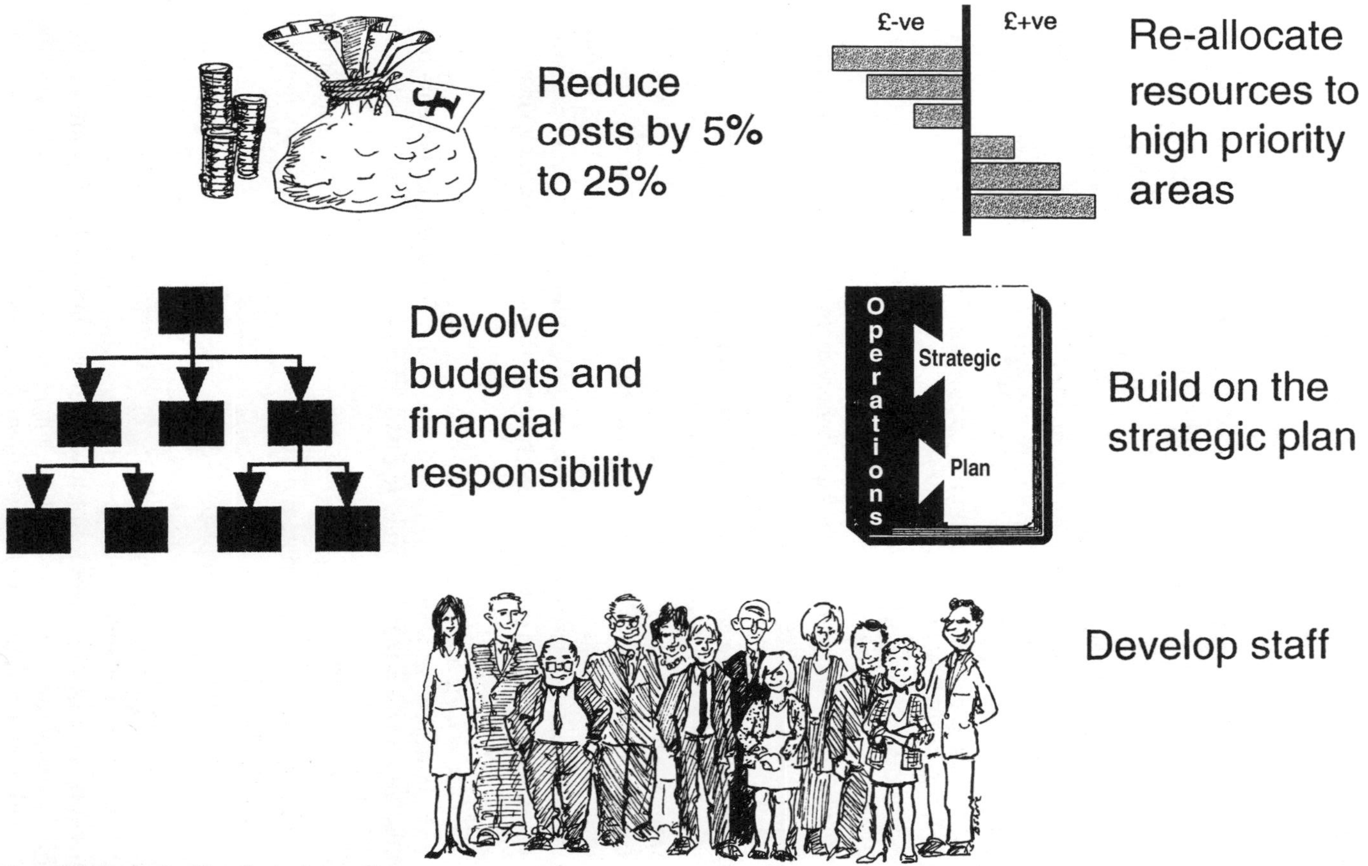

Re-allocate resources to high priority areas

£+ve

£-ve

Reduce costs by 5% to 25%

Build on the strategic plan

Strategic

Plan

Operations

Devolve budgets and financial responsibility

Develop staff

Fig. 7.1 Typical objectives: benefits

WHAT ARE THE POTENTIAL BENEFITS?

As mentioned, PBB delivers both hard and soft benefits to an organisation. Typical benefits and objectives are outlined in Figure 7.1.

Specifically, the hard benefits PBB has delivered in recent years include:

- **cost reductions** ranging from 5 per cent to 40 per cent. For example, 5 per cent in a hospital, 15 per cent in a local council to 40 per cent in a shipyard;
- **strategic plans** that were glossy but impotent pristine publications sitting unread on manager's shelves but can now be translated into the means by which staff understand the business environment and the pressures that they specifically face in their section and the steps necessary for the organisation and their section to take to move forward over the next few years and so achieve both their objectives and the organisation's;
- **budgets set**, both for the individual group and for the entire organisation in a very open and democratic but top management led process that encourages the support of staff. Examples include the Post Office, the Civil Aviation Authority, London Borough of Islington, Courage Brewery;
- **resources re-allocated** from the areas where there is lower business need for the services provided (often coincident with the manager who argues loudest and longest) to the areas with higher business need for the services. Examples include resources moved from paediatrics to porters, finance to IT, or street cleaning to creches. See Figure 7.2 for an example of re-allocated resources;
- **improvement in services delivered** in terms of a better match with what the customer wants. The customer (internal and/or external) is offered a range of services that each section could provide, stepping up from the minimum required to meet legal or operational needs and building up in realistic, incremental steps to a level of service that is greater than the present level of service delivered.

HOW DO YOU DO IT? THE PBB PROCESS

PBB process – overview

The PBB programme comprises five stages:

    I   Planning
    II   Analysis
    III   Improvement
    IV   Final proposal
    V   Implementation

Of these five stages, Analysis, Improvement and Final proposals are the core PBB stages, while the two additional stages, Planning and Implementation, are common and vital to all improvement programmes.

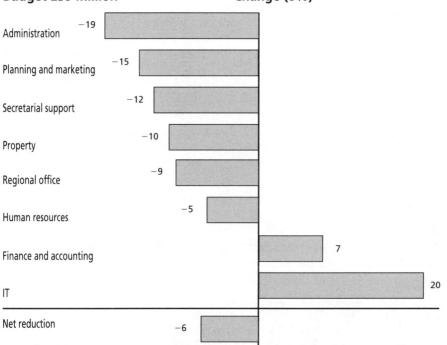

Budget £39 million   **Change (0%)**

Administration	−19
Planning and marketing	−15
Secretarial support	−12
Property	−10
Regional office	−9
Human resources	−5
Finance and accounting	7
IT	20
Net reduction	−6

Fig. 7.2 Benefits: re-allocated resources

Figure 7.3 outlines the PBB process in terms of these five stages with the core PBB stages broken down into an additional seven steps.

The Planning stage, undertaken usually in confidence, confirms the objectives of the programme, how these objectives can be met, i.e. the approach, who should be involved and what they should do. These elements are confirmed by the high-level steering group that contains the 'Great and the Good' from the organisation. Before kicking off, it is essential that very thorough planning has taken place to ensure that the PBB snowball is moulded in the right initial shape, starts rolling in the right direction and has the right people pushing.

Following training of all participants and a communication programme that publicly launches the programme, the Analysis stage determines 'Where are we now?' (Activity analysis) and 'Where do we want to be?' (Planning guidelines).

The Improvement and Final proposal stages are concerned with 'How can we get there?' Each area, using various tools and techniques and with the assistance of the project team, considers 'What services do we provide and what services should we provide?' (To be Effective); and 'how should we

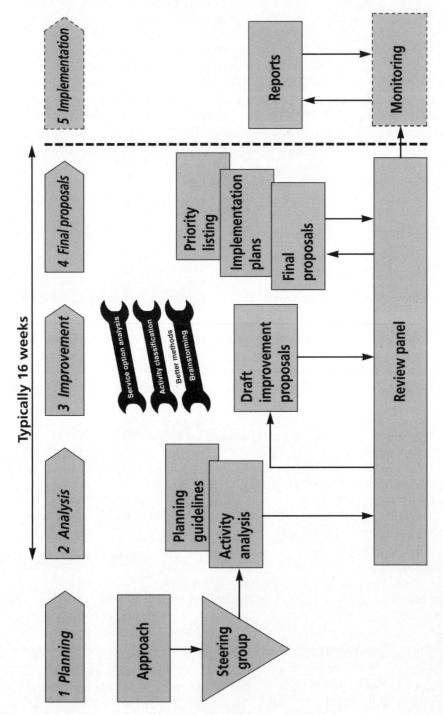

Fig. 7.3 Stages of the PBB process

provide these services?' (To be Efficient). A large number of ideas are generated in response to these questions and evaluation of these ideas begins.

The implementation stage aims to turn the paper benefits identified during the programme into real changes. This is achieved by summarising all the actions resulting from the programme, the steps required in each action, the person responsible and the timetable for each step. In addition an effective monitoring system is set up to measure and enforce progress. Having been all the way through the process (a lot of blood, sweat and tears, and a surprising number of laughs) it is essential to have a rigorous and disciplined implementation stage. It is too easy to run out of energy just when all the savings and other changes have been identified (on paper) and just when the final push is required to turn these paper changes into changes that the finance director would recognise and be able to measure.

The next section discusses each of the five stages in more detail.

PBB Process: Stage I – Planning

Don't kick the hornets' nest until you know what you are going to do next

This stage can take anything from six weeks to six months depending on the urgency and commitment of top management. The aim of this stage is for the steering group to agree an approach that will meet the objectives of the organisation. It is important that the organisation does not move forward until this stage has been effectively completed.

Specifically, during the planning stage you need to:

- set the objectives and scope of the programme including:
  - the organisation's **mission statement** including the purpose of the organisation and what benefit it provides
  - the **specific objectives** for the programme
  - the **main assumptions** that must apply such as for example the workload, the overall quality criteria, computer system X will be in place, etc.
  - **options** that should be evaluated, e.g. less demarcation, shift working, computerisation, etc.
- decide how the programme should be rolled out across the organisation; i.e. pilot, all at once, waves or a rolling programme;
- decide who will be involved, their roles and responsibilities;
- decide the coverage, i.e. what costs (staff and non-staff costs are included in the review, and what are excluded). In general all costs that can be influenced within perhaps two years should be included; fixed costs, i.e. those costs that it would be impossible or very difficult to influence can be excluded e.g. rent, rates, insurance;
- coverage is defined in terms of budget subjects. These generally mirror the

existing budget areas within the organisation. For the purposes of the programme, some budget areas are combined, split or excluded altogether. The resulting subjects represent conveniently sized units with a reasonably homogeneous group of services and a clear purpose;

- agree the timetable. Typically sixteen weeks for the analysis, improvement and final proposal stages. If the period is much longer the snowball loses momentum, actions would merely remain in the pending tray, if much shorter there would not be the time to do the work and the pressure would be excessive;

- tailor the approach. Although the general structure does not vary greatly from one application to another, the tools and techniques employed during the improvement stage in particular should be selected to address the particular needs and character of the organisation. Rather like a recipe, by changing one or two ingredients, the amounts of each ingredient or the cooking method or time, different results can be achieved of basically the same dish. Changes to the recipe are not made because of the whims of the chef but rather in response to the wishes or nature of the clientele – you, your staff or your organisation. Are they vegan, vegetarian, fussy or foodies, or are they tough or tender, ripe or unripe?

- decide upon a communication programme that will rapidly, effectively and honestly inform all the organisation about what is going to happen and begin to assuage unjustified fears as well as confirm real risks;

- develop training material and deliver training to all participants. This is the launch.

PBB Process: Stage II – Analysis

Where are we now and where do we want to be?

Step 1: The activity analysis determines 'Where are we now' by representing what staff **actually do**, what they produce, how they use resources (both staff and non-staff) and what these activities cost.

The budget subject manager prepares his activity analysis which is then discussed and refined in a workshop. The analysis typically sets out:

- the annual budget in terms of staff numbers, staff costs and non-staff costs;
- how staff time is used;
- facility and equipment usage and output analysis;
- costing of major outputs or services;
- the users of those services.

Step 2: At the same time the senior manager prepares for each budget subject planning guidelines, drawing from the organisation's overall planning guidelines and translates these for use at the subject level, to provide a framework for subject managers at the next stage. Additional objectives, assumptions and options can be included by the subject manager with agreement from the senior manager. These subject guidelines:

(a) set out the objectives for each budget subject for the improvement programme;
(b) define the core assumptions that must apply;
(c) describe the purpose of each budget subject and the benefits it delivers to the organisation as a whole;
(d) identify options that should be evaluated when considering better methods.

In this way, the organisation's strategic plan for the planning period under review is clear and concise – the organisation's overall planning guidelines. This then is cascaded down to all parts of the organisation as subject planning guidelines.

Step 3: the review panel (the Great and the Good for each particular area under review) reviews the planning guidelines and activity analyses to ensure a consistent and appropriate course is being followed for the next stages.

PBB Process: Stage III – Improvement

How can we get there?

It is during this stage in particular that the ideas for improvement are generated, building on the work completed in stages I and II. This stage is often about 'looking at things differently'.

Step 4: Subject managers undertake a radical re-appraisal, against the objectives set for them of what services they provide and how they provide these services; are there better methods that could be used to provide these services? Improvement workshops are run to assist subject managers. These workshops include customers of the service, peers, and colleagues.

Service option analysis

One of the tools that is frequently employed is service option analysis. Each subject manager identifies for their area a minimum or basic level of service. This basic level is usually defined by statutory or safety criteria or as the lowest level of service that would still enable the subject to fulfil its purpose, albeit poorly. Levels of service are then built up from this basic level in small steps so that there may be two or three intermediate levels of service before the current level of service is reached. The level of service is then increased beyond the current, so identifying rational and desirable enhanced levels of service. Figure 7.4 provides an example for a catering department.

Catering

Minimum		Room and hot water
	1	Sandwiches and drinks
Intermediate	1	Self service hot lunch
	2	Self service hot breakfast
Enhanced	1	Greater menu choice
	2	Waiter/waitress service

Fig. 7.4 Service option analysis – an example

The Improvement proposal sets out the two areas of work being undertaken:

(e) the review of potential better methods of providing services;

(f) the review of what level of service should be provided.

This distinction between method changes and service options is vital. A horror story that is often quoted is that of General Motors back in the 1970s which decided to introduce robots and computers into all their plants. They invested $40,000,000,000; sufficient to purchase Toyota outright. At the end of their investment, productivity had dropped rather than increased. The reason was because they had simply automated the wrong things; they were doing the wrong things right!

Figure 7.5 presents an Improvement proposal for a secretarial service, in diagrammatic form. The left side is concerned with doing things better. A long list of potential good ideas are being evaluated and categorised into:

(g) **assumed** – these are good ideas which will enable services to be delivered at less cost;

(h) **possible** – these may be good ideas but there has been insufficient time to assess them as yet;

(i) **rejected** – the idea is in fact a worse method of providing the service.

The right side of Figure 7.5 indicates service options. The secretarial services manager has decided that, at the minimum, only important reports actually have to be typed, everything else could remain hand written. If only this basic level of service was provided this would cost £255k and require fifteen staff. The next most important service level would be to type internal memos. This extra service would cost an additional £21k and require two staff. An enhanced service that customers are seeking is for a guaranteed 24 hour turn-around which would cost £15k and require one extra staff. Note the original budget was £300k and eighteen staff. The current level of service can now be delivered for 92 per cent of the current budget as the method changes have identified 8 per cent of savings. Thus if it was agreed that an enhanced secretarial service was in the interests of the organisation, this enhanced service could now be provided for £291k or 3 per cent less than the present budget. Clearly we have presented an ideal situation in order to illustrate the point; however this was taken from a real case.

Step 5: The draft improvement proposals are presented to the review panel to identify areas requiring clarification or further evaluation. At the review panel, each subject manager highlights the key points of his/her papers. The panel members ask questions to satisfy themselves that:

- all potential improvement opportunities have been identified;
- the opportunities being recommended are sound;
- any opportunities rejected have been rejected for valid reasons;
- opportunities requiring further evaluation will be progressed in a definite time period;

1. Method changes   2. Service options   No.   £ (000)

1. Method changes	2. Service options		No.	£ (000)	
Assumed • Standard letters • Answering machines • Filing clerk 8%	B	Important reports	15	255	85%
	C	Internal memos	2	21	92%
	B	24 hr turn-around	1	15	97%
Possible • Electronic mail • Typing bureau	Total proposed		18	291	
Rejected • Typing pool	Original budget		18	300	

Fig. 7.5 Improvement proposal: benefits

- a true basic service level has been identified and incremental services have been built up from this level;
- changes match the direction of the hospital's strategic plan.

PBB Process: Stage IV – Final proposal

What precisely are we going to do, what services are we going to provide and what will they cost?

Step 6: Subject managers finalise their improvement proposals taking account of the advice provided at the review panel meeting.

Step 7: The final proposals are reviewed by the Review Panel. As each manager presents their potential levels of service ranging from the basic up to enhanced levels of service, the review panel considers each level of service in turn and rates how important that service is to the organisation as a whole. The rating scale used is shown in Figure 7.6. Typically, basic service levels will score an 8, 9 or 10, with higher levels of service scoring progressively lower scores. All service levels from all subjects across the organisation are rated in this manner by the review panel.

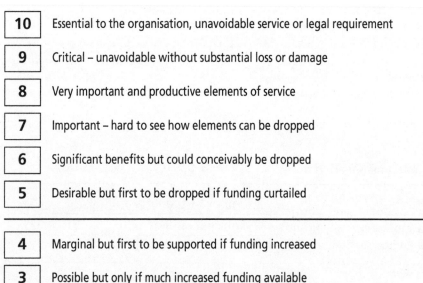

10	Essential to the organisation, unavoidable service or legal requirement
9	Critical – unavoidable without substantial loss or damage
8	Very important and productive elements of service
7	Important – hard to see how elements can be dropped
6	Significant benefits but could conceivably be dropped
5	Desirable but first to be dropped if funding curtailed
4	Marginal but first to be supported if funding increased
3	Possible but only if much increased funding available
2	Doubtful – not sufficient justification at present
1	Unlikely ever to be funded

Fig. 7.6 Service rating scale

As all service options are ranked in this manner, an overall listing of all services in priority order can be produced. Subsequently, recommendations can be made for funding in each subject and for the organisation as a whole.

PBB Process: Stage V – Implementation

Implementation of changes needs to be swift, effective and managed to cause the minimum of disruption to the organisation. This requires the identification of:

- the individual with overall responsibility for implementation;
- the steps required to implement, and individual responsibilities for each step;
- the start and finish date for each step;
- the personnel implications of implementation;
- the means to monitor progress against this plan.

The steering group agrees the implementation plan for each change, checking for consistency and the identification of dependencies. The project team monitors implementation against the plan, and reports to the steering group only where plans are not being achieved.

Who gets involved and what do they do?

The PBB programme tries to involve as large a proportion of the organisation's human resources as possible. See Figure 7.7. Potential specific roles include:

- Steering group member;
- Review panel member;
- Senior manager;
- Subject manager;
- Project team member.

In addition to these formal roles, staff are included on brainstorming sessions, training sessions and workshops as appropriate.

The review panel:

- reviews and approves planning guidelines, choice of subjects and activity analyses;
- challenges improvement proposals, identifies areas requiring clarification or further evaluation;
- reviews and ranks service levels and makes recommendations for funding;
- is set up with members that will enable it to:
  - have the knowledge and authority to review the subjects

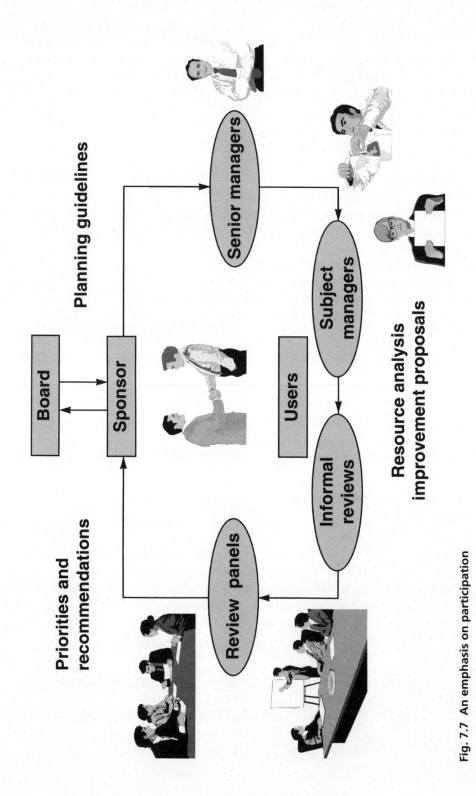

Fig. 7.7 An emphasis on participation

- evaluate both the providers and customers of service view
- spread the workload
- include some independent thinkers.

GOLDEN RULES TO HELP ENSURE SUCCESS

Drawing on the experience of applying various tailored versions of the PBB approach to some 100 organisations from both the public and private sectors, a small number of golden rules are evident that if applied properly should ensure success. This list of requirements is an essential list, and you need to be confident that they are all firmly in place or catered for before proceeding.

The cost of proceeding without any of these requirements is a significant drop in the morale of your staff and the waste of perhaps 10 per cent of the time of all senior, middle and junior managers over three to four months plus the cost of facilitation and project management. It is probably worth calculating this potential cost for your organisation before deciding to proceed – it helps to focus one's mind, and the chief executive's!

Golden rules include:

- **clear objectives at the start** – a small number of 'SMART'; Specific, Measurable, Achievable, Relevant, and Timed objectives. Typically no more than three. Define them clearly so that at the end of the programme you can clearly measure how well it has gone; i.e., rather than 'to improve morale', put 'to improve the morale of staff so that at least 60 per cent respond positively to a random survey questionnaire to be circulated in six months' time';
- **top management commitment** – don't believe the 'Yes, Yes we're right behind you, let me know how it goes' school of commitment. Commitment means making sufficient time available, typically 5 to 10 per cent of Board time (half a day a week for four months and a full day on three or four occasions). Typically top management will include the finance director, personnel director, chief executive, and operations directors of all main functions, for example in a hospital the nursing director, clinical director and directors of the key clinical services. This management team will need to decide that this programme is the highest priority. As it is not possible to go on adding work, it helps to ask what has been dropped off the bottom. If top management fail to make the time available, the programme will first lose direction and then fail as others involved in the programme follow suit and fail to make the necessary time;
- **prior briefing and training** – whether it's external or an internally driven programme, rumours will be flying before you even thought it possible. They are unlikely to be happy rumours as staff will feel threatened. You

need to counter-balance the image of a team of ten grey-suited, unsmiling accountants marching in step, armed with laptops, flip charts and knives bursting through their front doors. Staff need to know why they are doing this, what would happen to the organisation (and by inference them) if they did nothing, what is going to happen, who is going to do what, what is the likely outcome, what is their part to play, do they have the right skills;

- **adequate resources, mainly management time** – the resource required is predominantly management time. A PBB programme aims to bring together the ideas, experiences, skills and effort of most of the senior, middle and junior management team plus substantial numbers of other employees, drawing on perhaps 10 per cent of their time over a four month period. If this time is not made available, the programme must fail. In addition to management time, a full-time project team is required plus a room, computers, flip charts, etc.;
- **participative process with facilitators** – whether it is facilitated in-house or externally, the role of facilitation is essential to ensure open thinking and the involvement of as large and broad a range of staff as possible in order to generate ideas and gain wide acceptance and commitment to changes. To some extent, everyone will be stepping outside their main area of expertise. They need to be helped;

"All under control, sir!"

- **effective project management** – the PBB programme is a big animal that needs controlling. The timetable is always testing, large numbers of people are involved and all sections must have undertaken specific actions to an acceptable level of quality, by specific dates and at exactly the same time. This can only happen if the project is very tightly but sympathetically managed.

Managing the project – what skills are required?

A well managed PBB programme sticks to its timetable, causes minimum disruption to staff and the operation of the organisation, obtains the maximum feasible input from staff over the period, retains or improves the morale of staff, generates as large a set of quality ideas and meets its objectives. To manage a PBB programme effectively requires skills in:

- planning;
- project management;
- motivation and persuasion;
- team building;
- training, coaching and counselling;
- facilitation;
- problem solving techniques;
- financial analysis.

Encouragement – getting people to do what they'd really prefer not to do

Do you have staff with the right interpersonal skills or, in English, the skills to help people to:

- understand what to do;
- do things that, if left alone, they would not do;
- let you know how they are feeling while they are doing it?

Forget the 'I've sent out three memos now and still Joe Bloggs hasn't produced anything' school of thought. Get real – no one acts on memos unless it's basically to do something they want to do and were going to do anyway.

Quite naturally, nearly all staff will initially resist the changes being put forward; I would, you would. If anyone is initially enthusiastic, be on your guard, they probably have their own agenda. Think yourself into your staff's shoes. Staff will resist your proposed changes for ten main reasons, each of which requires a strategy to defuse or minimise the impact:

- **loss of control** – don't impose, discuss and gain agreement otherwise you risk staff feeling something is going to be done to them;

"It's a piece of cake, honestly."

- **excess uncertainty** – so provide information;
- **surprises** – so avoid them, provide information and timetables;
- **broken habits** – so provide reasons why change is needed;
- **the implication that the past way was wrong** – so make it clear (if true) that the past ways were right given that environment but now the environment has changed so the way things are done must change;
- **'you can't teach an old dog new tricks' syndrome** – so show how 'we've managed before', build up confidences and provide training;
- **disruption to plans and projects, 'This is all I need now, what with the XYZ project just starting up'** – so identify what projects, be flexible, build into programme if possible, or make clear what has priority;
- **more work** – so admit it, there will be but also indicate the reason for doing it. Try to identify for all groups of staff and individuals, their WIIFM – the What's In It For Me 'ism;

- **past resentments** – so discover the history, old scores and politics and develop a plan with specific actions that will build upon positive factors and help to neutralise negative ones;
- **real threats, e.g. job loss, power shifts** – so be honest. If redundancies are likely, say so, show how the process is fair and indicate what would happen if you do nothing.

Some common criticisms

During a programme such as this and with the luxury of hindsight at the end of the programme, various complaints always emerge. The skill is to be able to distinguish between the important and the tedious!

Important complaints require action to remove the cause of complaint, however others are more a symptom of human nature and there is little that can and often should be done about them other than to simply smile, nod and agree!

Common criticisms include:

- this is just a form-filling exercise. Correct, forms are used throughout the process in order to ensure the right information is produced, only the right information and set out in a common, succinct and comparable format. No one likes to fill in forms, this is a fact of life;
- 'the savings were identified on paper but somehow many never really emerged'. There is a real danger of this if insufficient attention is given to the implementation plan. It is vital not to let this happen;
- 'thank goodness that's over (PBB) now I can get back to my real job'. This is a very frustrating and frighteningly common comment that stems from managers failing to realise that the efficient and effective use of resources in their area is a central responsibility of theirs;
- 'hard work'. It is. This is rarely appreciated sufficiently at the start.

CHAPTER 8

Competition and partnerships

INTRODUCTION

In the preceding chapters several performance improvement techniques have been described. In pursuit of reduced costs and improved services, these have largely focused on internal restructuring of activities. Where external comparisons are made, they are usually indirect and focus on identifying benchmarks as targets to be achieved or exceeded. Competition through market testing and outsourcing are different; they confront activities directly with competition by inviting outside organisations to bid for the work.

TERMS OF PARTNERSHIP

Before describing the market testing and outsourcing processes, it is worth considering why, in some cases, competition leads to more efficient and effective services. The assumption is that the type of competitive forces which act on most activities in the private sector are similar for activities in the public sector. An exception may be made for functions that are proper to government, such as legislation, regulation, and the exercise of the judicial power of the state. Even in these areas, care must be taken to distinguish functions close to the heart of government, and those that really only give support.

Competition drives organisations to provide their services more efficiently and to be constantly improving quality. It is widely reckoned that competition is strongest where there are:

- a large number of organisations competing equally to provide services;
- few barriers to deter new organisations from entering the industry;
- service users (customers) with strong bargaining power;
- suppliers to service providers with countervailing power;
- the presence of effective substitutes for the product or service.

In the past, these have not typically been characteristics of public sector activities. Consider an in-house operation. Normally, there is one internal service provider, and outside firms are not, or more often cannot be, considered by departmental users. Anyway, users may have little incentive to drive down costs, if spending on the service is not charged directly to their units or if the cost is small in relation to their overall spending. The main suppliers to the operation are the people who work in it, and established practices, reinforced by inflexible pay and grading structures, may constrain change. Add to this a lack of low-cost substitutes, and it is not surprising to find a department paying for a costly, uncompetitive and possibly mediocre service.

This leads to opportunities for improving performance in at least two ways:

- changing the way services are currently provided by opening them up to external competition through outsourcing;
- exposing a current in-house service provider to competition from outside suppliers through a market test, as a spur to performance improvement.

Competition through market testing and outsourcing can be an effective tool for improving the value for money of public services. Both methods lead to a change in the focus of public service managers from **provision** of services to their **procurement**. This can be challenging: managers need new skills; for example, in specifying requirements and managing contractors, and applying strategic judgment in identifying the scope for involving the private sector.

COMPETITION AND OUTSOURCING

It is important not to lose sight of the fact that the purpose of competition or outsourcing is to secure better long-term performance of the services. The focus is on obtaining outputs cost effectively to a defined standard. There are two main options:

- **market test** – where the cost and quality of operations performed in-house are compared with what the private sector can offer through a competitive tender and the service placed with the provider – public or private – offering best value for money;
- **strategic contracting out** – where a decision is taken to outsource the provision of the service through a competitive tender without a market test of the in-house provider.

Candidates for market testing are likely to be activities where a competitive market exists, and the in-house activity has not previously been exposed to market forces. In certain cases an in-house bid may not be considered appropriate, and strategic contracting out of the service without a market test is going to be more fitting. For instance a view may be taken that:

- there is strong external competition for a large but fragmented service and in-house bid preparation would require significant restructuring;
- the quality of the current service is such that it would not be in the public interest to invest what can be substantial amounts to bring it up to a competitive level;
- the requirement is small and peripheral and it would be profligate for the public sector to continue to provide the service itself;
- the private sector has the capacity to provide services which could not be obtained as efficiently within the public service.

STRATEGIC SERVICE REVIEW

These possibilities mean that it is essential to conduct a full review of the service – and the market to provide the service – to determine the most feasible and productive way forward. Market testing exercises can be costly where an in-house operation has to be transformed to become more effective, and this highlights the importance of identifying where strategic contracting out is the better overall choice.

However, an in-house bid does give an incentive for strong competition on price. Private firms are conscious that they must beat the bid of the in-house team. Consequently there is a tendency for lower prices when an in-house bid is expected. Under the UK government *Competing for Quality* programme, percentage cost savings have averaged 8 per cent higher when services were contracted out after a market test than when an in-house bid was not submitted.

It is therefore vital to analyse the existing service properly and examine the market to provide the service. Fundamental questions need to be asked:

- do we need the service at all?
- are there parts of the service which we will not need?
- how much does it currently cost to provide the service?
- does the current service provide what we need?
- what is the type and level of service we want?
- are there private service providers with the capability and interest to provide cost-effective service?

It is important that the service review focuses on the service that will be required in the future. A large central government department identified its information systems (IS) training branch as a suitable candidate for market testing. The branch employed over 70 staff. Before embarking on the market test, the service was reviewed and client departments were consulted on their future IS training requirements. Changes in the structure and size of the department and the forthcoming implementation of its IS strategy led to the conclusion that there would not be a large core requirement for IS training in the future. The market test did not proceed, but the exercise identified a staff reduction of over 50 per cent.

A comprehensive service review should:

- determine broadly the size and scope of the operation;
- identify the resources that are currently used in the operation so that its cost can be calculated;
- consult service users to determine the present level of customer satisfaction with service levels and standards and their possible future requirements;
- conduct a basic market review to gauge the interest and capability of firms which could provide the service;
- plan in outline how to submit the work to open competition.

At the end of the service review, the options for the way forward should be clear. Managers should have a good idea of the type, scope and level of services that will be needed with the relevant costing implications. They will be able to set out ways to package work in a way that will present an attractive opportunity to the market and deliver value for money.

THE COMPETITIVE TENDERING PROCESS

The competitive tendering process must follow well established good public procurement practices. The key principles are:

- ensuring fair competition and equality of opportunity for all suitably qualified tenderers;
- employing a competitive process to obtain best value for money for the purchaser;
- establishing a contractual agreement between the purchaser and provider of services.

CONTRACTING FOR PUBLIC SERVICES

A contract is a means of allocating risk between the purchaser and a contractor providing services. The greater the risk borne by a contractor, the higher the price, but the lower the likelihood that the purchaser will have to pay for any price variations if risks materialise. Conversely, if the purchaser agrees to bear the risk of unexpected events, the contractor will charge a low fixed price but expect to be paid for any work which is not specified in the contract. A purchaser seeks a balance between carrying risks and paying for them if the risks occur, and the benefit of a truly fixed price.

Whether embarking upon a market test or a strategic contracting out, the exercise must be governed by good public procurement practices. Public procurement law exists which lays down procedures that must be followed for all but the smallest of contracts. It sets out requirements for advertising, the selection of bidders and criteria for the award of contracts. The laws also mean that if a specification is drawn up in such a way that only one provider can in fact provide the service, then this is unlawful and could be challenged in the courts. Table 8.1 gives a summary of the procurement law which covers contracting for public services.

Determining tender strategy

Decisions must be taken about the way in which work will be presented to invite competitive bids. This is known as the tender strategy. Different options can greatly affect the nature of the competitive tendering process because different approaches vary in their attractiveness to potential contractors. Sound decisions must be made about:

- **size of contracts** – factors which determine the size of contracts, such as volume of work, geographical coverage, organisational boundaries, must be appraised to assess the advantages and disadvantages of having one or more contracts;
- **scope of the contract** – the use by a contractor of publicly owned assets will be among the factors which affect the scope of the contract. Accommodation and equipment should normally be offered to external contractors on the same basis as they are offered to in-house teams;
- **type of work included in the contract** – it is often both advantageous to the purchaser and attractive to contractors to combine one or more functions in a single contract package. This is sensible where activities are similar – for example, typing and secretarial services – or where one activity is dependent on another, such as operating a large computer system and providing maintenance to it. Putting together different functions gives contractors the opportunity to achieve economies of scope and scale, and offer innovative ways of providing the service;

Table 8.1 Public Procurement Law

In the UK, the applying to public procurement of services is embodied in the Public Services Contracts Regulations 1993 which implemented the EC Public Services Directive (92/50/EEC). Among the main features of proper public procurement are:

objective evaluation	the use of objective criteria for selecting bidders in awarding public sector contracts and award procedures that make clear to all interested parties the basis on which a contract is awarded;
equal opportunity	publication across the European Union of information about public sector contracts, so that potential suppliers throughout the union have equal opportunity to tender for public sector contracts;
non-discrimination	there must be no discrimination between one potential contractor and another nor against contractors from other member states of the European Union on grounds of nationality;
no competitive barriers	technical specifications which may discriminate against certain national suppliers in the European Union are prohibited, as these effectively act as barriers to trade.

For some services, large but manageable contracts may be attractive to potential bidders, but for others – where the industry is unaccustomed to contracting for large packages – large contracts may deter bidders. One central government department invited five private-sector firms to tender for a three-year contract to provide typing and secretarial services to around sixty offices across the South West of England. The size and scope of the contract package was unattractive to the private sector, and none of the private firms chose to bid against the in-house team of staff.

- **pricing basis** – the basis on which the contractor will be paid should give contractors an incentive to improve both efficiency and performance and give the purchaser a high degree of certainty about cost. For this reason a lump sum, with a proportion linked to performance targets, is attractive, but where work volumes are expected to vary widely, prices will have to be linked to the amount of work produced by the contractor;
- **the contract duration** – short contracts, for two years or less, are not usually attractive for purchaser or contractor. The contractor's initial costs (for example, to invest in equipment or to recruit and train staff) have to be spread over a shorter period, which increases the contract price. More frequent tendering is also costly for the purchaser.

Selecting bidders

The process of selecting bidders – private firms who will be invited to bid for the work being offered – has two main aims:

- to generate wide interest in, and competition for, the contracts from firms who have a capability to undertake the work; and
- to reduce the costs of tendering, both for the purchaser and for external firms.

Generating interest in contracts improves competition for the work being tendered. The greater the number of external firms that express an interest in tendering, the more opportunity the purchaser has to select a number who are likely to be capable of delivering the service. Also, if wide interest is encouraged, the competitive tendering process is more open and fair.

Not every potential contractor who expresses interest is invited to tender. Instead, a short list is normally prepared. Shortlisting limits the number of contractors who are invited to tender. This makes evaluation of the bids received more manageable and less costly. It also avoids a large number of contractors incurring abortive costs from preparing unsuccessful tenders.

Bidders are selected from those who express interest as a result of advertising. There may be a requirement to place a notice in the Official Journal of the European Community (OJEC). Advertising in the national, local and trade press also helps to ensure that the potential field of possible bidders is explored. It is the most effective way of making sure that the maximum number of potential bidders are aware of the contracts.

Generally, no more than six contractors should be chosen to submit bids. The selection should be based mainly on an evaluation of information given by each contractor about its capability to perform and complete the contract. Interested contractors should be asked to give information about their:

- company status;
- financial stability;
- technical ability.

Preparing tender documents

The preparation of the tender documentation is the most exacting and time-consuming phase of the process for the purchaser-side team. The main tender documents are:

- **specification** – describing the services to be delivered;
- **conditions of contract** – defining the binding agreement between the purchaser and a contractor;
- **invitation to tender** – setting out the procedures with which contractors have to comply to make their bids;

- **tender schedules** – prescribing the information which bidders are required to present in order to submit a full tender.

The specification is usually the most detailed and important of the tender documents. A specification must be based on users' requirements and not dictate current processes and work methods. It is essential to incorporate the service standards that are desired. A good specification is not prescriptive about the resources to be employed or the methods to be used, but will describe the requirement in terms of:

- the functions to be performed (scope of service);
- the outputs sought (quantities);
- the performance required (quality).

For example, a courier service could be defined in this way as 'a service to handle an average of 100 items despatched each day' (function and quantity) 'and deliver 95 per cent of all items within 24 hours and all items within 48 hours' (performance).

Writing a specification is a key activity in the overall competitive tendering process. It is a major task, particularly when a large amount of data about the service has to be collected, often for the first time, in order to define the outputs that are required. In addition, where the activities to be tendered are large, complex or especially important to meeting the objectives of the purchaser, wide-ranging consultation and agreement may be needed.

Inviting tenders

Contractors on the select list are formally invited to tender by sending them the tender documentation. The preparation of tenders is an intensive and demanding activity for bidders. Consequently, adequate time has to be given for contractors to prepare their bids. During this period, it is important that all dealings with bidders are conducted on a fair and equal basis. Strict guidelines must be adopted for dealing with approaches from contractors. An important principle is that all bidders should be provided with the same opportunities and information. This means that every effort must be made to see that all bidders receive equal treatment and identical information.

The arrangements for giving additional information to bidders during the tender period must be clear, and apply equally to all external bidders. As well as providing information to bidders in the tender documentation, bidders may be given further details at briefing meetings, site visits or in response to their questions. The aim of giving information to bidders is to equip them to understand the service requirement fully, so that they can tailor their offer to give the maximum benefit to the purchasing organisation.

Setting performance standards

Good performance standards may be specified and measured in several ways:

- **accuracy** – the proportion of outputs that should be produced that are flawless or within acceptable, defined limits, e.g. the percentage of incorrectly typed words in a randomly selected sample of typing output;
- **timeliness** – the number of occasions when outputs are to be delivered on time; this may be expressed as a proportion (%) of the total, e.g. the percentage of accounts settled within a target time period;
- **availability** – the number of occasions when the service is demanded and is to be available, normally expressed as a proportion (%), e.g. the percentage down-time for a computer system;
- **responsiveness** – the maximum time to be taken to produce a satisfactory outcome compared with a pre-set target; this is often expressed as a proportion (%), e.g. the percentage of callers to a help desk who have to wait more than a certain time;
- **customer satisfaction** – the level of satisfaction expressed by customers, users or recipients of the service, measured in an independently conducted survey.

Preparing a specification

- prepare a plan for producing the specification;
- produce and agree an outline structure for the document;
- identify the information that has to be collected;
- prepare a profile of the service;
- review and set performance standards with users of the service;
- define the service in terms of the results and performance required – try to avoid being too technical and prescribing inputs, resources and processes;
- write the specification in plain language and try to avoid technical or official expressions;
- consult users of the service at each step to ensure that the specification meets their requirements;
- get the specification approved in good time for incorporation in the tender documentation.

Market tests – the in-house team

Unless the service is being contracted out without a public-sector bid, then an in-house team will be busy while the purchaser is preparing for the competitive tender. Usually the in-house team will be made up of staff involved in currently providing the service, supported as needed by additional internal resources or external consultants. Its attention will be on organising internal resources to create a competitive operation – and this task is at the heart of market testing as a tool for performance improvement.

To achieve the necessary transformation into a competitive service provider, in-house teams will need to employ many of the performance improvement techniques described in the previous chapters. This will entail a process of:

- **producing a profile of the existing service** – defining what services are provided, with what resources, for whom and to what purpose;
- **assessing the full cost of the current service** – establishing a base for reducing costs, making comparisons with external providers and setting bid prices;
- **identifying business improvements** – developing proposals for delivering the services in new, more effective ways;
- **preparing a business plan** – producing a realistic and achievable plan for developing the in-house service into a competitive operation.

The in-house team also has to develop its bid for the competitive tendering process. An indicative bid, covering both the in-house team's price and technical proposal, must be prepared in advance of receipt of the formal invitation to tender from the purchaser. This is based on the team's understanding of the current service and its costs, and incorporates planned improvements from the business plan. An astute team will consider alternative service-level options so that, once it receives the specification with the invitation to tender, it can adapt its indicative bid for the formal tender.

Preparation for in-house teams

- establish a team to prepare for and compile the in-house bid;
- enlist any wider expertise needed from within or outside the organisation;
- analyse the current methods and procedures for delivering the service;
- assess the full costs of all the resources needed to deliver the current service;
- identify areas for performance improvement to create a competitive service offering;
- gather information about potential competitors and their strengths and weaknesses;
- prepare a realistic and achievable business plan for implementing the new service;
- produce an indicative bid based on a revised costing and the proposals for a more effective operation;
- establish the core members of the bid team;
- when the ITT is received, read the documents carefully to determine exactly what is required;
- adapt the indicative bid to produce a final tender complying with the purchasers requirements;
- produce a professional and well presented tender submission document;
- submit the tender on time and in accordance with the instructions for tenderers.

Selecting the contractor

Strict formal procedures should be followed by the purchaser for the receipt and opening of bids. This ensures that all tenders are treated equally and there are no opportunities for carelessness or impropriety.

After tenders have been received, bids are evaluated to identify the successful contractor. This part of the process, tender evaluation, focuses on three different aspects of each contractor's bid:

- compliance with the tender conditions;
- assessment of technical capability to deliver the service;
- financial evaluation of bid prices.

Detailed procedures are followed to evaluate bids. An evaluation team systematically reviews each bidder's ability to undertake the work and prepares a thorough and fair assessment of the cost of accepting each bid.

Following evaluation, tenders are compared and the contract awarded. The process of tender evaluation is complex and does not rely purely on financial comparisons. The purchaser is looking to find the best value for money, and this does not necessarily mean acceptance of the lowest price.

Following the decision on award of the contract, successful and unsuccessful bidders are notified. If the award is made to an external contractor, a contract is signed and the contractor mobilises its resources to start. When an in-house team is successful in a market test, the formal arrangements are set out in a Service Level Agreement (SLA). This establishes the working relationship between the purchaser and the in-house contractor.

Managing the contractor

Once the service contract has been awarded, effective contract management is essential to ensure that the prime objective of market testing and outsourcing – to achieve value for money – is actually attained. Contract management involves the control and monitoring of a contractor's performance from the day on which the contract takes effect. It is the responsibility of the purchaser and continues throughout the period of the contract. Among the key aspects of successfully managing a contract are:

- regularly checking that service standards are maintained, and that the operation is effective and customers are satisfied with the service they are getting: giving the contractor feedback on performance is essential;
- ensuring that payments to the contractor accurately reflect the services actually provided and that all variations in the contract are formally agreed with the contractor;
- assessing the services and the value for money obtained with a view to re-tendering when the contract period expires.

STRATEGIC PARTNERING

Both public and private-sector organisations have traditionally bought goods and services on the basis of competition. The view is that the best value for money is secured by treating suppliers adversarily and through competition involving regular and extensive contests amongst a large number of suppliers, mainly on the basis of price. But more and more, purchasers are realising that their suppliers are vital to the service they deliver. In the motor industry through just-in-time supply arrangements, and in many retail firms through co-operation with manufacturers, strategic purchaser–supplier partnerships have become best practice.

Strategic partnering recognises the problems conventional procurement incurs:

Monitoring contractor performance

- agree and set up the client-side organisation to control and monitor the contract;
- appoint a contract supervisor, confirm their responsibilities and notify the contractor who it will be;
- inform customers and users of the service of their responsibilities with respect to monitoring the new contractor;
- agree with the contractor the content, format and frequency of its performance reports;
- arrange monthly review meetings between the contract supervisor and the contractor's manager;
- following the start of the contract, undertake regular and random monitoring of the contractor's performance;
- follow up customer complaints with the contractor;
- make payments to external contractors only when the work claimed for by the contractor has been assessed and verified;
- undertake ongoing reviews of the service levels and service standards;
- amend the contract or service specification by issuing variation orders;
- keep comprehensive records and proper files detailing the delivery of the service and recording dealings with the contractor;
- periodically review user satisfaction and the development of the service to prepare for the eventual competitive re-tendering of the service.

- **significant procurement costs** – regular competitions and the need to maintain contractual relationships with a large number of suppliers is a significant overhead to the business;
- **variable service quality** – the greater the emphasis on price competition the greater the risk of poor service quality or service failure amongst suppliers.

This has led to new approaches to purchasing by reducing the number of suppliers dealt with regularly and changing attitudes to purchaser–supplier relationships. Emphasis is placed on working together with a few select suppliers over the long term to reduce the cost of supply and improve service quality. It has also led to a growing recognition that suitably motivated suppliers can make a wider contribution to their purchaser's business.

The contrasting characteristics of conventional relationships and a partnering approach are shown in Table 8.2. The two approaches are very different. A significant change in both working practices and culture may be needed to accommodate partnering arrangements – in both the purchaser and supplier organisations. The main characteristics of partnering contracts are trust and openness in a way that makes explicit the way the contract is functioning and reduce the risk to both parties. This is achieved in some or all of the following ways:

- **open book accounting** – revealing the costs and income associated with the contract. This requires the ring fencing of accounts associated with the contract to make profits or losses evident to both parties, and contractors may install accounting systems that allow direct access by the purchaser;
- **benchmarking** – providing a basis for price renegotiation, although it may need to be supported by an arbitration process in the case of disputes. It also encourages the contractor to adopt best practice in service provision, and needs to be associated with a savings or profit sharing scheme;
- **savings sharing** – a system of rewarding the contractor for cost savings delivered to the purchaser. The aim is to encourage innovation by the service provider and deliver savings to the purchaser during the period of the contract. Care is taken to ensure that the purchaser still receives the

Table 8.2 Conventional supplier management arrangements vs the partnering approach: key characteristics

Conventional supplier management	Partnering approach
• Large number of suppliers	• Small number of suppliers
• Regular competition on the basis of price	• Infrequent competition – use of benchmarking as an alternative
• Tightly drawn short-term contracts	• Memorandum of agreement geared to encouraging flexible and long-term working relationships
• Adversarial/arms-length relationship between client and supplier	• Joint working relationship based on mutual dependence, respect and trust
• Suppliers form a relationship with the client's purchasing/ contracts functions	• Suppliers form relationship with all levels of client management
• Client employs large purchasing/ contracts function to manage suppliers	• Small 'purchasing' function geared to working with suppliers
• Supplier and client operate separate quality control arrangements	• Supplier's quality management systems are integrated with client's
• Supplier involvement in client's business (outside contract) not sought	• Supplier involvement in many aspects of client business encouraged
• Restricted flows of information between client and supplier	• Exchange of information between client and supplier
• Emphasis of financial control on short-term supplier price	• Emphasis of financial control on long-term total cost of supply

quality of service required, and that the contractor's overall level of profitability is protected;

- **profit declaration** – contractors declare the level of profit they expect to gain from the contract. In return they expect a similarly open approach from the purchaser to help reduce the level of risk associated with what would otherwise be unpredictable changes in the volume or form of services required;
- **information sharing** – the purchaser brings the contractor into its planning process and shares information and thoughts about how its needs may affect its need for contracted services;
- **length of contract** – a contract of at least five years' duration, preferably with an option to extend subject to satisfactory performance. Contracts usually contain clauses giving the right to terminate the contract for substantial non-performance.

Partnering arrangements between the public and private sector are not yet extensive. Consequently, the successful operation of this kind of arrangement is of extreme importance to private firms. They wish to demonstrate both that they can deliver high quality services to the public sector and that they accept modest gains through a long-term relationship with a purchaser rather than higher, but less predictable, gains through contracts subject to regular competition.

Selecting the strategic partner

Advertisements in the press or the OJEC may reveal a large number of suppliers who claim to have skills and expertise in a particular service area. Sifting out those with appropriate technical expertise in the service area should be straightforward. The process of identifying a supplier with the best cultural fit, in having complementary skills and expertise and in their approach to partnering arrangements, is less easy. The chance of success is greatly improved by carefully preparing the ground in advance of any advertising. In particular, by ensuring that:

- **a partnering approach is fully justified** – a strategic service review informed by the decision tree shown in Figure 8.1, must be conducted before any partner selection exercise begins. While the procurement exercise should not stifle innovation, any potential for confusion amongst potential partners about the objectives of the exercise should be avoided. For example, if a partnering arrangement is being sought, then potential partners should be told that the conventional market test option, involving an in-house bid, has been ruled out;
- **ideal partner attributes are defined** – an analysis of the strengths and weaknesses of the existing service provider should be undertaken so that

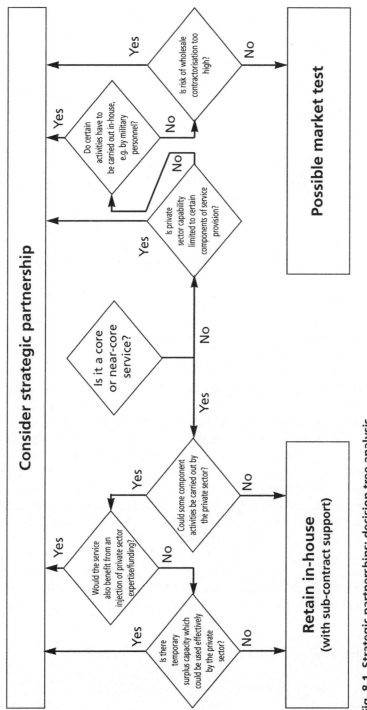

Fig. 8.1 Strategic partnerships: decision tree analysis

the matching attributes of an ideal partner can be established – these provide the basis for criteria to subsequently evaluate tenders;

- **an outline development plan is prepared** – this will outline the tasks and performance improvements expected of the partnership and will be developed in consultation with potential partners. However, it is important that the purchaser provides an initial framework for these discussions;
- **clear and concise information on the current method of service delivery is available** – although the specification supporting any partnering arrangement should be output and not input based, as much information as possible should be given to suppliers on current methods of service delivery, resources and potential constraints to process re-engineering. The ability of potential partners to suggest innovative but practical improvements to working methods is improved by giving information;
- **the appropriate procurement route is chosen** – depending on the value of the contract and service characteristics, the requirements of the EC Services Directive will have to be followed in selecting a partner. Deciding on which of the allowed procedures to adopt – restricted or negotiated – will depend on the following factors:

  - need for negotiation – the EC Directive states that negotiated procedures should be used where the requirement is insufficiently clear at the outset to permit 'prior overall pricing'. In practical terms the more opportunity that exists to explore innovative solutions and working arrangements with potential partners the more likely the right partner will be selected
  - time available to select a partner – negotiating can extend the selection process by several months: time which may not be available if the organisation is under pressure to meet performance reporting timescales
  - need for a start-up phase – even with the benefit of negotiation it may be impossible to arrive at a well defined (and priced) long-term contract. In these circumstances a two-phase contract can be awarded. The first phase covers a short period for the selected partner to work with the purchaser to develop a detailed performance improvement plan. In this case the selection process focuses on selecting the right partner rather than the financial details of the second and longer phase of the contract. Such an approach allows the suitability of partners to be tested during the first, trial, phase of the contract.

MAKING PARTNERING ARRANGEMENTS WORK

Having selected the partner, arrangements must be made for the partnership to develop and flourish. This needs:

- mechanisms to encourage private sector commitment and participation;
- a contract which is geared to a partnering arrangement;
- contract and service management arrangements.

Figure 8.2 illustrates some of the aspects of making a successful partnership work. Above all, a balance must be struck between:

- providing sufficient flexibility and freedom of action to encourage innovation;
- incorporating adequate controls both to monitor partner performance and to guard against service deterioration or failure.

Service standards	Managing process and culture
• Well defined and measurable • Performance reports monitored in a constructive fashion • Working together to set new/improved performance standards • Emphasis on outputs and not delivery mechanisms	• Client focus on problem resolution not problem identification • Client places reliance on suppliers' quality control system • Board-level representation/commitment • Both parties receptive to change, and suggestions for improvement • Share tactical and strategic information • Client encourages innovative proposals
Roles and responsibilities	**Incentives for contractor**
• Clearly defined • Change is, however, recognised	• Commitment to a long-term relationship • Incentive pricing • Opportunity to expand range of services

Fig. 8.2 Making the partnership work

Encouraging partner commitment

With a substantial stake in a new business, a private-sector partner will expect to work closely with the existing management team. In practical terms the partner will expect:

- senior board-level representation with a right to attend all board/management meetings;
- the roles and responsibilities of staff from both parties at all levels of management to be clearly defined through a process of joint consultation and agreement;
- a well defined process for performance monitoring, review and issue resolution to be established;

- access to technical, operational and financial information on all aspects of the business;
- an input to decisions affecting the performance of the business as a whole (as well as those decisions directly affecting those activities for which the private- sector partner is directly accountable).

The existing management team will need to respond positively to these requirements and hence may have to adopt a more open and participative style of management. They may also need to develop a greater commercial awareness if they are to respond effectively to their partner's proposals for change.

Providing the contractual framework

Although some private-sector partnering arrangements are based on an agreed statement of intent rather than a very detailed and legalised contract, it is difficult to envisage public-sector partnering being based on anything other than existing government contract conventions.

However, care must be taken to ensure that a contract reflects the aims of the partnership, and in particular does not constrain the development of a close working relationship where the skills and abilities of both parties are used to their maximum advantage. As a guide, contract and supporting documents must be based on the following:

- **a statement of the objectives of the partnership and how it is intended to operate** – the private-sector partner will be expected to make a major contribution to the objectives of achieving significant cost savings and performance improvements or both;
- **a service specification which is output and not input or activity based** – the private-sector partner's innovative ideas and skills, for example in process re-engineering, must not be constrained by a tightly drawn specification;
- **a clear and unambiguous statement covering the relative roles and responsibilities of both parties** – the contract may need careful wording to accommodate year-on-year changes in the relative responsibilities of both parties;
- **statements indicating how an effective joint working relationship will be achieved** – by reference to rights to attend board meetings and senior management performance reviews, right of access to strategic and tactical information, and agreement on procedures for actioning proposals for changes in service delivery mechanisms;
- **incentives to achieve performance improvement targets** – consideration should be given to some form of arrangement whereby cost savings are shared, or additional bonus payments are made to the private-sector partner on the achievement of performance improvement or financial targets.

Managing and controlling the contract

Partnering arrangements should not be seen as soft or easy options. Although an open and trusting relationship is required for the partnership to be successful, this does not mean that the controls associated with effective contract management can be disregarded. If anything, the process of control will need to be reinforced by using:

- **a detailed action plan** of what the partnering arrangement is to achieve, how it is to achieve it and by when, to monitor progress – this is developed in consultation with the selected partner during the negotiation process but will need to be constantly reviewed and updated;
- **a clear and concise definition of service standards** against which performance will be monitored – no different from a conventional purchaser-supplier relationship;
- **a reporting mechanism** to ensure that these performance standards are rigorously monitored and that any shortfalls are fed back, to the other party, in a constructive manner;
- **an arrangement for sharing information, ideas, and proposals** to identify areas for service improvement – regular monthly meetings to discuss tactical issues, less frequent meetings to discuss strategic issues, annual meetings to develop the action plan based on the service requirements for the following year;
- **an auditable cost recording system** operating in accordance with agreed definitions of unit output costs, overhead allocation methods etc. The credibility of such a system is critical where a profit or cost-savings sharing regime is to be operated and essential to provide clear and documented evidence for payments by the purchaser to the contractor.

STRATEGIC PARTNERSHIPS – THE FUTURE?

Partnership styles of working between the public and private sector will continue to grow in popularity. They provide a framework to bring together the strengths of both sectors, share risks and provide a much broader access to funding for both small and large scale projects. By the year 2000 we envisage partnership working to be an integral part of the public service managers portfolio. We anticipate this being the norm in most advanced economies.

CHAPTER 9

Corporate transformation

INTRODUCTION

The preceding chapters in this book have been concerned with individual performance management techniques, the relationship between them and how to use them. We have stressed the need to tailor each approach, and indeed to mix and match between them, where necessary, to meet the requirements of each organisation.

However, having read about each of the approaches available, and having considered the best usage and the strengths and weaknesses of each, you may be thinking that:

- no one approach is broad enough to meet the requirements of your organisation, even with the tailoring we have described – you may for instance feel that there is also a need to look at the role of your IT, or your approach to marketing (if relevant), or reward structures;
- even with the help of the diagnostic assessment in Chapter 2 you cannot really identify the performance improvement needs of your organisation, because its strategic direction, and thus the performance improvements required, are unclear.

We increasingly find in the course of our consulting work that organisations need to step back and assess their overall position, so that they can frame clear strategies and objectives for their corporate performance, and address the full breadth of their business activity. If there is a fundamental challenge, either some threat or opportunity, the required response may be bigger than just business process work, or cost management, or cultural change, alone. What is needed is a more integrated response, which:

- identifies where the organisation currently stands;
- validates – or re-defines – its direction and strategy;
- identifies the business changes which are required to make the transformation, programmes these according to business priorities and justifies them in terms of costs (if necessary), risks and benefits;
- configures the different performance improvement approaches, and also others such as IT strategy, to deliver the changes in the programme;
- implements these changes and delivers the benefits sought;

- establishes the framework of performance measures which will keep the organisation 'on track' thereafter.

Within this framework it is possible effectively to re-invent the organisation. Because it is so wide ranging, we call it, 'Corporate Transformation' (or when used in the context of public service delivery it could be better described as 'Government Transformation'). The rest of this chapter sets out the different stages involved, and how it might be applied.

WHAT IS CORPORATE TRANSFORMATION?

To an extent, transformation is a matter of degree – it represents change that is certainly wider, and probably more radical, than could be achieved by any one of the techniques described earlier in this book. However, we have found that there is a certain threshold beyond which change is qualitatively different. Thus, we define a transformation as:

> . . . an integrated response to fundamental challenges to the purpose of an organisation, where the organisation develops; execute and sustain a programme of radical improvement to the performance of processes and people.

The external challenge will be sufficiently fundamental to require *significant* change to most *and possibly all* of the organisation's existing purpose, strategy, objectives, processes, systems, structures, costs, business methods, core competencies and culture. At the extreme, the organisation has to re-invent itself. It follows that the change required will be wider than could be achieved through any one 'point' approach (such as BPR or ABM) or even, say, pairs of these in simple combination. Transformation will involve tailoring together *multiple approaches* to deliver the specific changes required by each organisation.

Transformation *commences at the strategic level*. It is difficult to transform an organisation without some vision to guide the activity involved. Not all transformations will require a fundamental change of strategic goals, but there is a need at least to challenge, re-examine and update any existing strategy. To achieve the transformation, the organisation will typically be led by a *strong central individual*, such as the chief executive officer (CEO), or sometimes by a *cohesive leadership team*.

FRAMEWORK FOR TRANSFORMATION

The main stages in the transformation process are shown in Figure 9.1, overleaf. Note that they are shown as sequential steps for clarity: in practice, steps may well overlap, and require some 'back-tracking' and iteration. Each stage is briefly discussed below.

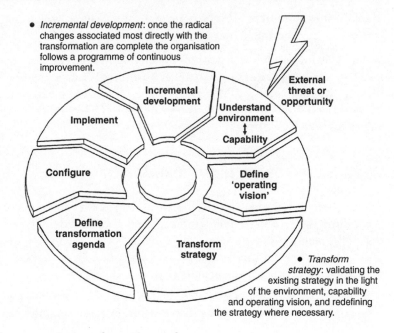

Fig. 9.1 The corporate transformation cycle

Understanding the environment – and yourself

Major change needs to rest on a clear understanding of the environment within which the organisation operates, and its internal capability to respond. This understanding needs to be shared sufficiently for a wide cross section of the organisation to grasp the need for change.

Transformation drivers

Our experience has shown us that, while there are a great many factors which will be relevant to a transformation, there are some particular transformation *drivers*. These are the factors which can either cause the need for the transformation, or make or break it by their presence or absence.

We have found eight possible drivers at work with our clients, shown in Table 9.1. The drivers work singularly or, more probably, in combination. As a generalisation, the first five drivers in the list tend to provide the stimulus (the opportunity or the threat); the latter two tend to determine how the stimulus actually triggers the change, and to influence the results. Leadership, in particular, is in our experience a critical determinant of the success or failure of transformations. The remaining driver, ideas, can operate in either capacity.

Table 9.1 Transformation 'drivers'

Transformation drivers	Examples of specific issues
Market	Customers: (end users, intermediate) Stated or anticipated needs and preferences – requirements for added value Market climate: How is the market changing? Growth/decline Globalisation – extent/implications Opportunities/threats Barriers to market entry/exit New markets
Competitors	Current competitors: Who currently leads the market? How? Competitors' strategies, strengths, weaknesses Own relative competitiveness (costs, quality, service, technologies, etc.), own strengths/weaknesses Potential competitors: Market entrants (strategies, strengths, weaknesses) Industry realignments Substitute products Organisations with similar processes, inputs, technologies
Regulatory	Sources of external regulation: Governmental, watchdog International (e.g. EC) Quality standards organisation Environmental Taxation Legislation Public opinion
Technology	New product and process technologies/trends New information technology/trends Application of technologies Suitability of existing technologies
Leadership	Recognition of relationships with stakeholders Dimensions of leadership: Style Proactivity Motivation Articulation of vision/communication
People	People dimensions: Culture Trust Flexibility/ability to change Skills and capabilities – core competencies

Table 9.1 – *contd.*

Transformation drivers	Examples of specific issues
Fundamental organisations	Merger, acquisition
	Privatisation, outsourcing
	Effectiveness of current structure:
	Ownership
	Capitalisation, funding
	Strategic fit of all components
	Group-subsidiary relations and controls
Ideas	New ideas
	Existing vision and strategy
	New vision and strategy
	Internalisation of ideas

Note that 'financial constraints', per se, do not appear on the list. While cost pressures can prompt a quest for greater efficiency they are unlikely, in our experience, to drive a radical transformation of the whole organisation. High costs may of course be causing a wider problem, such as uncompetitiveness, but the transformation driver in this instance is the competition, and not the cost situation in itself.

When assessing transformation drivers, the key questions to ask are:

- what threat or opportunity is driving your requirement to transform?
- how well understood are the drivers in question, and how widely – is the *need* for change accepted by those affected?
- how do the drivers inter-relate with each other?
- how effective is the existing leadership style (a difficult question to ask if you *are* the leader of the organisation, but a critical one none the less)?
- what are the prospects if we do *not* transform ourselves?

Transformation 'resources'

In addition to the transformation drivers, there are a series of other factors which need to be taken into account when understanding both the external context and the internal positioning relative to this. These other factors cannot cause, or make or break a transformation in the way that the drivers can, but are likely to provide the *content* of the transformation programme. We call these factors transformation resources.

Table 9.2 shows the key resources which we have identified from our work with clients (some will not be relevant to public sector organisations). The 'understand' phase of the transformation process would need to develop a

Table 9.2 Transformation resources

Resource type	Examples of specific issues

Products	Products/services mix:
	    Primary
	    By-products
	End use

Inputs	Raw materials/processed inputs:
	    Availability
	    Cost/quality/timeliness
	
	Suppliers:
	    Performance, flexibility
	    Relationships to date/required
	    Trading practices
	Labour market

Activities and processes	Cost-effectiveness, quality, service levels, responsiveness, etc., of:
	    New product creation
	    Demand creation
	    Order fufilment
	    Purchasing, storage and distribution
	    Other processes
	Methods, technologies in use
	Internal structure of organisation

Finance	Cash position
	Cost structures:
	    Activity/process costs
	    Product costs
	    Overhead costs
	Working finance:
	    Cash, overdrafts, loans, equity
	Treasury management

Physical assets	Plant machinery, land, property
	Knowledge:
	    Market knowledge
	    Patents/IPR

Shareholders	Shareholder value added
Other external stakeholders	Community stance, impact/relations Political stance, impact, relations Environmental stance, impact, relations

Management style and practices	Established practices, processes:
	    Project management style
	    Line management style
	    Control philosophy and systems

Table 9.2 – *contd.*

Resource type	Examples of specific issues
People in the workplace	Work unit climate
	Motivation
	Reward systems
	Individual needs and values
	Skills
Performance management	Performance measures in use:
	Processes
	People
	Functions, branches
	Quality, effectiveness, relevance
	Style of use
	Performance levels achieved:
	Absolute and relative (e.g. benchmarks)
Linkages	***How do drivers and resources interrelate?***

high level view of where the organisation stands against each of the resources shown.

Most performance improvement techniques focus on 'activities and processes', and the cost aspects of 'finance': the range of additional issues illustrates the potential breadth of impact which a transformation may have. In particular the application of performance measures will be critical:

- do the measures translate from strategic objectives into usable targets for processes, functions and people?
- given that 'what gets measured gets done', are you measuring the right things – are the measures prompting the *right* behaviour to meet the organisation's goals?
- do they provide a suitable management information base on which to monitor the performance of the organisation and take corrective action?

Setting the vision

If an organisation is to sustain a process of major change such as a transformation, it will need a picture of the end-point to sustain it. We call this the 'operating vision'. This should describe, in terms which make it accessible to everyone in the organisation, what the organisation will be doing, how it will do it, and what it will be like to work for, once the transformation is complete. Staff 'buy-in' to the vision is a critical step in the process of managing the changes likely to be required.

The previous step defined the need for the transformation; the vision expresses what the transformation will be *to*. It should capture the aspirations of the organisation in a way which is accessible to the staff who will deliver them. In contrast with the 'hard' factual analysis and investigation of the previous stage, the process of defining the vision should seek to tap the spontaneous and intuitive energies of those staff, whether through brainstorming workshops or other techniques.

There are many possible ways to express the vision. For example:

- a 'day in the life of' the organisation's customers, managers, staff, suppliers and other stakeholders;
- scenarios for possible futures;
- key principles which will govern conduct and operations;
- what the new 'heresies' will be.

Key questions are:

- does your organisation have a vision which has engaged the energy of its staff?
- does it define the end-point for the transformation in a way which is accessible to the staff who will deliver it?
- does it position the organisation appropriately given the factors assessed in the previous stage – is it sustainable?

Will the existing strategy deliver the vision?

The next stage in the transformation cycle is to assess the applicability of the existing business strategy to deliver the transformation. The operating vision defined the end-point – what the transformation will be *to*; the strategy should define in broad terms *how* it will get there by defining strategic objectives and critical success factors.

The business strategy may need to be revised or completely replaced if:

- the 'understand' phase throws up issues which the current strategy does not take account of, or which make it invalid;
- the visioning stage defines an end-point which the existing strategy will not deliver.

The definition of business strategy is a subject which has been the subject of many books in its own right, and it is not proposed to emulate these here. In the context of a transformation, the key questions will include:

- is there a clearly defined business strategy, and how clearly and widely is this communicated?
- will the strategy address the issues identified in the 'understand' phase, in particular the transformation drivers, and will it deliver the vision mapped out in the previous phase?

- does it provide a basis for identifying the priorities for change and allocating resources?
- does it specify organisational level objectives or critical success factors which can be used to derive performance measures throughout the organisation?

If the answer to any of these is 'no', then there will be a need at least to update the strategy before proceeding to specify the changes which will achieve the transformation.

What is the business agenda for the transformation?

The transformation agenda is the sequenced set of business projects which when implemented will deliver the transformation in line with the strategy defined in the previous phase. In this sense the transformation agenda is the 'implementation plan' for the transformation – it is where the analysis and conceptualisation of the previous stages begins to turn to action.

The emphasis is on *business* projects at this stage of the transformation cycle. Examples would be:

- 'revise service mix to achieve . . .';
- 'improve service delivery processes to achieve . . .';
- 'achieve a total quality culture . . .';
- 'revise our IT strategy and infrastructure in line with . . .';
- 'improve overall efficiency and effectiveness by . . .'.

The configuration of the different performance improvement approaches to achieve these business changes – in other words, how BPR, ABM, TQM, PBB and the rest would be deployed to achieve these – is covered in the next stage.

Most transformations will take a relatively extended period of time, and the organisation will pass through several interim stages before the change programme is complete. What should these stages be? For example, should the organisation's cost structure be tackled before its business processes, or in parallel? How does this fit in with the extension to its IT strategy which may be required? What will the organisation look like as each stage is completed – how much will its performance have improved from the previous stage, and in what respects?

The agenda which results will be unique to each transformation, but will be based on a balance between a number of criteria:

- the time available to the organisation to complete its transformation – there is little point, for example, in planning to take three years if you are due to be privatised in one;
- the short and longer term importance to the business of each element on the agenda;

- the benefits which result at each stage – there may for example be a need to free up benefits at an early stage to cost justify the whole programme;
- the balance of risk which results at each stage;
- the fit of the different components together – for example, if cost reduction and other BPR work are required, it may be sensible to construct a single process map of the organisation as the basis of both exercises;
- external legislative or policy constraints;
- change initiatives which may already be in hand, and their relationship with the transformation (for example, should they be discontinued, should they be absorbed?);
- the rate of change implied by the programme and the balance between the extent to which the organisation (and its staff) can accommodate this, and the need to sustain momentum.

The progress of the transformation will need to be tracked. A further role for the transformation agenda is therefore to specify success criteria and performance measures to allow this to happen.

Finally, the agenda will also set out the programme management arrangements for the transformation as a whole.

Configure

This stage is where the different performance improvement approaches, together with others such as IS (Information Systems) Strategy, are configured to support the business projects in the transformation agenda.

The stage requires considerable knowledge of these approaches in order to identify:

- areas of synergy – for example, if a transformation requires a combination of IS Strategy, BPR and cost reduction, it would make sense for them all to use the same process map of the organisation;
- potential conflicts – for example, where a functionally based cost management technique such as PBB reinforces those functions just as BPR attempts to take a process view which requires them to be broken down;
- interface requirements – for example ensuring that process maps are developed in sufficient detail, and in the right way, to support any systems design work which may be required.

The systems issue apart, many of these considerations have been covered earlier in the book. However, in the context of transformation, the breadth and extent of the required tailoring and configuring will be significantly greater. There is also a need to interweave the change management actions required throughout the programme to ensure that the changes which result are understood and accepted by those affected.

As each project in the transformation agenda is configured, it should be possible to write a taut scoping document combining the results of this stage and the previous one, and setting out:

- the business purpose of the project and the expected benefits;
- success measures;
- its role in the transformation programme;
- the approach to be used, with tasks and timings;
- management arrangements, including the interface with the overall management of the programme;
- interfaces and dependencies with other projects;
- skills and resource requirements;
- costs and risks.

Implementation – 'doing it'

This stage represents the delivery of the transformation 'on the ground' – the achievement of radical changes across the breadth of the organisation. Clearly, each implementation will be specific to the organisation concerned, and it is accordingly difficult to generalise in a book of this nature. However, there are likely to be the following broad stages:

- **analyse** – assess the detailed implications of the strategy which has been adopted, assess in detail current processes, systems, culture and organisation, and also identify quick wins;
- **design** – identify the detailed implications of the Operating Vision for processes, systems, organisation and culture, and propose changes;
- **establish** – gain approval and buy-in, define implementation projects;
- **realise** – actually making the changes which will deliver the required benefits (system development, process changes, organisation changes, people changes, etc.).

In practice, implementation activity is likely to start in some areas before others, and will thus overlap with the preceding configure phase – the process is not as sequential as the corporate transformation cycle in Figure 9.1 might imply.

The stage would conclude with the implementation of the framework of measures for processes, functions and people to allow the organisation to be managed once the transformation is complete.

Incremental changes

This final stage marks the day-to-day improvements which the organisation will continue to make once the main phase of the transformation is complete.

CHAPTER 10

Focusing for success

INTRODUCTION

In this book we have outlined a range of performance improvement methods for public service managers. New challenges will emerge and priority issues will continue to change. Cost pressures may come and go as government policy changes, the private sector will probably continue to take on more and more of the tasks traditionally undertaken by mainstream public sector, and as more information about service levels becomes available managers will be under the spotlight to secure world class performance. To respond, managers need to focus on the real needs of the situation facing them.

FOCUS ON YOUR REAL NEEDS

Your organisation's agenda, needs and objectives must be paramount – not what a standard approach or technique dictates – if it isn't right for you don't use it!

In selecting a performance improvement option, the public service manager should ensure there is clarity defining the real problem to be addressed.

Managers should consider the following issues:

- focus on what needs to improve – and ensure that everyone has the same understanding of the problem;
- define why it needs to change and how urgently – is there a compelling reason to change the way things operate?
- select technique for the job in hand;
- tailor technique for your own purpose and objectives;
- don't window shop for acronyms;
- don't image that because an approach worked elsewhere it is automatically for you;
- ensure that the project has the right level of support and own the project and changes.

'Change will not happen automatically'

In any performance improvement project, the team must always remember that simply going through the process of technique will not in itself bring about improvement. Real improvement will only be realised if the project changes the procedural or structural way of operating. Performance improvement projects can have profound effects on the way the organisation operates, both in terms of what staff do from day to day and how the organisation structures itself to deliver services. This impact should never be overlooked and it should not be assumed that change will automatically happen.

We have already addressed the point that change will not happen automatically – real and long-lasting improvement will only happen if the organisation and people within the organisation understand and change their behaviour to reflect the change.

Figure 10.1 shows that change is a process in its own right with a start and end-point and a transition state. The transition state typically has the following characteristics:

- low stability;
- high emotional stress for the project team and those that are affected by the change;
- high, often undirected energy.

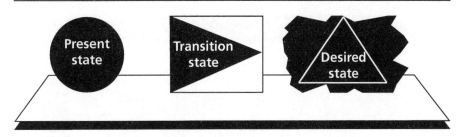

Characteristics of the transition state:

- Low stability
- High emotional stress
- High, often undirected energy
- Control becomes a major issue
- Past patterns of behaviour highly valued
- Conflict increases

Fig. 10.1 Implementation – change is a process

At this time, control becomes a major issue and a clear direction and vision must be shared by the organisation. Barriers to implementation of changes are shown in Figure 10.2. Most of these barriers can be overcome by thinking through and properly planning the implementation of change.

FINAL THOUGHTS

If we were to reflect on the key messages we have tried to communicate to you through this book, we would like to leave you with what we see as the fundamentals:

- be driven by your own objectives and organisation's needs;
- don't be afraid to put together your own performance improvement technique – picking the best from each of the approaches;
- never ignore the impact on the people within your organisation.

Challenging it can be – frustrating often – but always rewarding when you deliver sustained improvement.

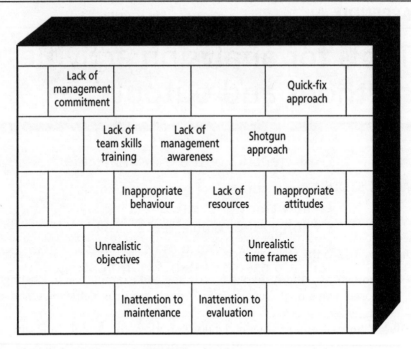

Fig. 10.2 Overcoming implementation barriers

Tools for analysing activities, methods and outputs

WORK STUDY

Work study is a generic term for the tools which are used to examine human work, to develop and improve work methods and to establish suitable standards by which the performance of work can be measured. It incorporates:

- **method study** – the systematic recording and examination of existing and proposed ways of doing work in order to improve efficiency and cost-effectiveness;
- **work measurement** – a collection of tools for establishing the time required to carry out a specific job at a defined level of performance. Work measurement methods may involve indirect time study (using a stop watch or other direct means) or indirect time study (using data from previous studies or other analytical/estimating techniques);
- **time and motion studies** – these combine elements of method study and work measurement and involve watching and recording the work carried out by staff in order to assess how efficiency may be improved.

ACTIVITY ANALYSIS

Activity analysis is the identification, measurement and analysis (in terms of time, cost and throughput) of the activities undertaken by people in an organisation. It is what staff do. Activities can be analysed:

- by business process which considers the activities involved in achieving a specific output or outcome and may cut across more than one department or function (this may also be referred as Process Analysis – see below);
- by organisation which identifies the activities undertaken by a particular department or cost centre;
- by function which considers the detailed activities within a specific function and which may span more than one department – this is particularly useful for systems design type work.

The most common approach is to analyse activities by organisation and then to consider whether there are key business/cross department processes.

Activity analysis can involve the identification of outputs and the calculation of activity and output costs. Under such circumstances the term is being used to cover both activity analysis and **Activity based costing** (see below).

Similarly activity analysis may incorporate elements of **Cost driver analysis** (see below) and **Performance indicators** (see below).

The scope of activity analysis can range from a simple analysis of an individual department, process or function to a detailed and comprehensive analysis of a whole organisation. The approach adopted and the documentation used needs to be tailored to the scale and complexity of the assignment in hand.

Activity analysis is an important tool in the following areas of work: performance improvement, organisational design, total quality (customer/supplier relationships), IT systems design, management information, process systems design.

Activity may also involve some form of **Activity classification** which can assist in identifying the core activities of the business and areas for potential cost reduction. Typical classifications are Primary/Secondary (P/S), Value Added/Non Value Added (VA/NVA); Discretionary/Mandatory (D/M); Core/Support (C/S) and Repetitive/Non-Repetitive (R/NR).

Process analysis

Process analysis is used to analyse and improve processes (a collection/sequence of interdependent activities) that span one or more departments/functions and which achieve a common purpose. Generally, processes are defined so as to take in a complete 'value chain' – for example, a complete purchasing process. This ensures that the processes span organisational divisions (in the example, stores, inventory, purchasing, goods inwards, billing and so on); which in turn maximises the likelihood of significant performance improvements being identified.

Process analysis is activity analysis approached from a process perspective. However, it may involve a number of specific techniques such as **process mapping, input/output analysis, 'from-to' matrices and process workshops. Process mapping** involves preparing a diagrammatic description of the main information and material flows of a process. It can be undertaken using a technique such as walk through.

Walk through or **Routing by walking about** involves walking the process to discover what actually happens rather than what is supposed to happen. For example, if the process is paying an invoice or processing a grant claim you would pretend to 'be' the invoice or grant claim, and would ask each person – including messengers and mail room staff – what they receive from the previous person, what they do with what they receive, and how long it takes, what they use to do it, and what they pass on to the next person. At the same time, questions can be asked about difficulties experienced, ideas for improvement, and so on. Walk throughs are time consuming, but a very effective way of finding out about process structures, and also of consulting all the staff involved.

Process analysis is an important tool for eliminating duplication, reducing process lead times eliminating wasteful activities, enhancing departmental boundaries/interfaces, restructuring organisations, and improving workflows. Process analysis is best performed interactively with client staff, in order to obtain their validation of any models created and ownership of the results.

Business process re-engineering is a comprehensive and wide-ranging methodology which incorporates process analysis but which is specially designed to achieve radical and significant improvements.

Performance indicator analysis

Performance indicators are collected and reviewed in order to assess:

- whether the organisation is aware of the key performance measures for activities/processes/functions;
- whether data is retained on key performance measures;
- whether standards of performance are improving or meeting targets and how they compare (see below) to best practice/other organisations.

In most organisations performance indicators cover the quality, cost and timeliness of activities and outputs.

Organisation analysis

Organisation analysis involves the review of organisation charts or organograms. These charts set out the organisational structure in terms of job titles, roles and relationships. The drafting/review of organisation charts can assist in:

- relating activities and outputs to the human resources used;
- making preliminary assessment of efficiency and cost-effectiveness;
- determining activity and output costs;
- assessing whether organisations are structured in the best way to support their business processes.

Computer modelling

Computer software packages can be used to assist in the documentation, analysis and simulation of business activities and processes in order to identify weaknesses/inefficiencies and to forecast the implications (costs and other outcomes) of different business strategies. Examples of the use of computer modelling in performance improvement are:

- to document processes and workflows and identify areas of weakness/inefficiency;
- to simulate changes to processes and workflows and to assess their operational implications;
- to support activity based costing;
- to calculate the financial implications of changes to working methods and cost structures.

There is a distinction to be drawn between the use of graphics packages to draw process models, and true modelling tools which allow data to be appended to parts of the model, and which support consistency checking between levels.

TOOLS FOR ANALYSING THE RELATIONSHIP BETWEEN ACTIVITIES, OUTPUTS AND RESOURCES

Activity based costing

A technique through which costs are related to activities and outputs and hence to the services provided to customers.

Activity based costing can range from a simple, one sheet analysis of the cost of activities undertaken by a group of staff (typically a function) to a comprehensive analysis of an organisation's activities installed on a database. This database may then be manipulated depending upon the assignment objectives.

Activity based costing can also be used to develop an **activity based budget** which sets out the resources required to produce a given level of output/service.

High level contact analysis

High level contact analysis involves estimating the costs of an activity or function using data which is already available and making generalised assumptions where data is incomplete. The information obtained provides a best estimate of total and unit costs but would need to be further refined if detailed costs comparisons/analysis are required.

Cost driver analysis

A cost driver is a factor which has a direct influence on the occurrence, and therefore the costs, of activities and business processes. Cost driver analysis involves investigation of these factors to identify the root cause (source) of costs.

Cost driver analysis enables an organisation to focus on those factors having the greatest impact on costs.

Cost driver analysis can be very easy and straightforward to undertake. However, in complex processes it may require several days of participatory workshops to identify the key cost drivers, to determine the costs associated with the cost drivers and to develop an action plan for reducing the impact of the cost drivers.

Budget data review

Budget data review involves understanding the composition of an organisation's budget and the relationship (as expressed in the budget) between costs and activities and outputs. This is an important tool for assignments involving cost reductions, the development of new budgets and the provision of improved management information.

TOOLS FOR ANALYSING THE EFFECTIVENESS/COMPETITIVENESS OF ACTIVITIES AND OUTPUTS

Benchmarking

Benchmarking compares the performance of an organisation/function with external standards. This enables areas of comparative weakness and the action required to improve performance to be identified. Benchmarking may be undertaken on the basis of costs/prices, staffing levels, productivity, service quality and systems and procedures. Benchmarking may be undertaken against a variety of criteria including:

- best in class; against firms with similar processes but not necessarily in the same industry;
- competitors, against direct competitors;
- industry, against other players in the industry but not necessarily direct competitors;
- internal: against other functions or departments of the same firm.

Benchmarking can involve a full formal comparison with other organisations or an informal comparison based on previous experience. The comparison can be at the level of performance measures alone; alternatively this can be used to guide a comparison of process structures and techniques used in order to explain how the performance differentials arise.

It is important to recognise that by itself benchmarking is meaningless. It needs to be accompanied by an analysis of processes and costs in order to help the organisation improve its performance where the benchmarks indicate it has scope to do so.

Repeated benchmarking over a period of time can be an important aid to fostering a climate of continuous improvement.

Customer/client surveys

The use of customer feedback from formal or informal surveys of satisfaction as a measure of the quality of services and to identify how improvements could be made.

The scope and complexity of the survey will depend on the results required and the number of customers/clients. The survey may need to be designed and undertaken by professional researchers. Alternatively, it may be undertaken by project consultants on the basis of telephone calls, interviews, workshops, lists of questions and by reviewing other documentation, for example records of complaints, previous customer satisfaction surveys.

SWOT analysis

Analysis of the strengths and weaknesses (internal factors) of any aspect of an organisation's business position and the opportunities and threats (external factors) which it faces.

Once the strengths, weaknesses, opportunities and threats have been identified, either on a one-to-one interview basis, or preferably through a workshop, the consultant may assist in generating ideas to build on strengths, alleviate or overcome weaknesses; take advantage of future opportunities and plan to investigate threats.

TOOLS TO DETERMINE HOW PERFORMANCE CAN BE IMPROVED

Analysis tools

The analysis tools identified under the heading *Process analysis* can be used to determine the areas in which performance needs to be improved. Many of the tools can also be used to identify how performance can be improved, for example work study, activity analysis, cost driver analysis and benchmarking.

Planning guidelines

Planning guidelines provide a framework for any performance improvement assignment, in that they set out the broad aims and assumptions of the assignment and in some cases highlight specific areas of concern. By setting them initially at the top of the organisation and then at each level down the organisation, they provide the means to cascade down through the organisation the aim, assumptions and options for change of the performance improvement assignment.

Planning guidelines should be set at the start of an assignment and modified as necessary during its course. Normally they consist of a purpose and benefit statement plus aims, assumptions and alternatives. The **aims** or objectives should comprise the quantified aims for the assignment, for example to improve performance by 10 per cent. The **assumptions** should identify those changes to the business environment that should be assumed as part of the project, for example introduction of new computer systems or new legislation. The alternatives should highlight key areas to investigate and opportunities to change or options to consider which guide the review process, for example contracting out, skill mix, increased use of computers, etc.

Ideas generation

A number of the analysis tools already discussed will involve the generation of ideas about the way in which performance can be improved. Two specific techniques for ideas generation which are particularly effective are:

- **visioning** – this involves assembling a number of people together to discuss views about the sort of organisation that they are seeking to develop in terms of its culture, management style, market position and overall aims and objectives. By developing a shared vision options for change can be identified which move the organisation towards achieving this vision;
- **brainstorming** – this involves assembling a number of people together to think through issues and seek group solutions in a non-critical environment. Brainstorming is based on the concept of synergy – the theory that by working together a group is greater than the sum of its parts.

Service-level analysis

A process of identifying the incremental levels of service and the associated resources for a discrete part of the business building up from the absolute minimum service. The service levels identified may be ranked in priority order against the incremental levels of service of other parts of the business.

Developing service-level options is a useful tool for reallocating resources in line with corporate objectives and priorities, reviewing how objectives are achieved and improving efficiency and cost-effectiveness. It is particularly useful in circumstances where there is choice about the level of service provided or the way in which it is provided, for example in priority based budgeting.

Priority listing/review panels

A process of performance improvement will require decisions to be made about changes to working practices and cost reductions. Some of these will require a straightforward (accept/reject) response but others will involve a thorough review of priorities and options. Key decision making tools include:

- review panels to review proposals for services and to establish priorities;
- a point scoring system which enables priorities to be established and uncovers misunderstandings or disagreements;
- a priority listing which sets out options as a ranked list of priorities.

Glossary of terms

Activity analysis	The analysis and measurement (in terms of time, cost, throughput) of distinct activities which go to make up a process. A number of tools and techniques can be used.
Benchmarking	Comparative measurements, comprising identification of the factor to be measured, identification and surveying of appropriate sources of comparison and sizing of the gap to be bridged.
Best in class	Benchmarking a specific process or activity against the best known exponent of that process or activity, most often a non-competitor in a different industry (also known as co-operative benchmarking).
Competitive	Benchmarking against direct competitors.
Industry	Benchmarking against other companies in your industry (including international) which may not necessarily be direct competitors.
Internal	Benchmarking against other functions, departments, divisions, units or companies within the same group.
Service	The benchmarking service includes all the elements of the basic definition above, but also includes the analysis of how to bridge the gap.
Brand	Title or device specific to one organisation that provides a mark of quality assurance.

	May open a single product, service or range of services.
Continuous improvement	Constant incremental improvement, usually implemented through an empowered work force.
Critical success factors	A measurable financial or operational factor, which is critical to the success of the organisation.
Culture	The deeper level of basic assumptions and beliefs that are shared by members of an organisation, that operate unconsciously and define in a basic 'taken for granted' fashion an organisation's view of itself and its environment. 'Culture' includes the way people behave towards each other and the rituals and routines of organisational life.
Hallmark	Distinctive style of service delivery which is recognised as a branch, e.g. Bain.
Methodology	Tool, technique or analytical framework needed to provide a service.
Objective	The point aimed at – defined in a measurable way.
Organisation	A system delineating the structure and reporting relationships between management positions. Organisation is the process of identifying and grouping work to be done, defining and delegating responsibility and authority and establishing relationships to accomplish objectives.
Plan	A detailed and co-ordinated set of activities required to translate a strategy into the actions deemed necessary and sufficient to realise its objectives.

Process	A set of logically related tasks performed to achieve a defined business outcome characterised by:
	– having customers for the defined outcome (internal/external)
	– crossing organisational boundaries
Core	A process which delivers those critical factors which give the business competitive advantage, i.e. those factors which are required for success in the industry and which the company strategy has identified as the most critical to focus on in order to beat the competition.
Mapping	Diagrammatic description of the main information and material flows within a process. This can be done hierarchically, starting at the highest/simplest level (Level 1) and then increasing levels of detail.
Simulation	Modelling (not necessarily computer based) of the process to evaluate 'what if' or 'what could be' scenarios. A number of tools and models can be used, e.g. SPARKS.
Support	A process which may not be central to delivering competitive advantage but which is critical in supporting those processes. Many head office overhead processes fall within this definition.
Product	(Internal) Components of a service which may be recognised by a client, e.g. activity based costing (as a component of a cost reduction service).
Quality	Of product, process or service – degree to which recipient's requirements are satisfied.
Total	A company-wide programme which focuses on customer–supplier relation-

	ships; empowerment of staff; costs of quality; defects prevention and so on.
Radical	A step change in improvement as distinct from incremental change often associated with continuous improvement programmes.
Responsibility	The liability to be called to account for actions and decisions taken, or for the overall performance of part of the organisation.
Service	Core service (benefit, output or change) recognised by the client. Example – **Post-acquisition integration**.
Category	Grouping of services/products into the main categories of business solutions required by clients. Each category being targeted at different levels and buyers in an organisation. Example – **Process design and improvement**.
Skill	Professional expertise in a range of services/products/ methodologies. Example – **Management accounting**.
Workshop	A group convened to focus on specific business issues and develop solutions.

Index

Glossary references are indicated by bold type.